AF270032

Praying the Parables of Jesus isn't just a book you read. It's a guide to a deeper understanding and experience of the with-God life. Step through it slowly. Savor it. And let God do his work as you live in his unshakable Kingdom.

Ted Harro, president of Renovaré

In *Praying the Parables of Jesus*, Macchia and Skinner prayerfully, methodically, and artistically share Jesus' parables with twenty-first-century disciples. They encourage readers to embrace a more intentional life of slowing down, thus experiencing greater comprehension of Jesus' parables and more in-depth intimacy with Yahweh. Lectio divina and visio divina are integrative devotional practices. What a blessed contribution to the faith-forming community.

Barbara L. Peacock, founder of Peacock Soul Care and author of *Soul Care in African American Practice* and *Spiritual Practices for Soul Care*

The parables of Jesus have a way of drawing us into the reality of the Kingdom he came to announce. What a gift this book is to help us pray these stories and embrace the "unhurried intimacies" to which Jesus invites us.

Alan AND **Gem Fadling,** founders of Unhurried Living, Inc. and authors of *What Does Your Soul Love?*

Praying the Parables of Jesus demands that we listen, with fresh attentiveness and seriousness and playfulness, to Jesus' stories and that we open ourselves wide not just to what he's saying but also to what he's doing. With simple, penetrating commentary and arresting, soul-searching illustrations, Macchia and Skinner have dreamed up and pulled off a conspiracy of transformation. If you want to keep Jesus at a safe distance, this is not the book for you. But if you're ready to have Jesus turn your world upside down, start here.

Mark Buchanan, author of the David Trilogy

The paradox of this beautiful collection of words and images is that Macchia and Skinner guide the reader deftly into restorative relationship with Jesus not by exhausting exegesis but by winsome invitation. It is a rare experience to have yourself shepherded in clear, sensible steps not to right answers but to our Savior. This book is a gift to all who are hurried and harried by the world and who long to have gentle and kind guidance into the disruptive, delightful rest that only deep encounter with Christ brings.

Tara Owens, founder and executive director of Anam Cara Ministries, spiritual director, and author of *Embracing the Body* and *At Play in God's Creation*

This is a delightful, intriguing, and creative invitation to engage with the parables. It's fresh and deep—as deep as you'd like to go.

John Eldredge, author of *Wild at Heart*

This is more than a devotional book—it's an immersive encounter with Jesus and his teachings. We are invited to linger in each parable, not just as readers but as participants through holy reading and holy seeing. The stunning artwork helps us see truth beyond words. This is a treasure to return to again and again.

David AND **Cindy Wu,** cofounders of Mosaic Formation

What an excellent idea! A careful devotional guide for a journey through the parables of Jesus. I can hardly believe that this classic method for stepping into the most important stories Jesus told has so rarely been the subject of a book. I highly recommend this devotional reading that is so well conceived and delivered.

Gary W. Moon, founding executive director of the Martin Institute and Dallas Willard Center at Westmont College and author of *Apprenticeship with Jesus* and *Becoming Dallas Willard*

If you long for fresh insights from Scripture, "unhurried intimac[y]" with Jesus, and encouragement to apply the Spirit's promptings to your daily life, then *Praying the Parables of Jesus* is for you. Be ready for surprise blessings! You'll walk with Jesus through a field and stumble on treasure. You'll knock on the door of his heart, receive fresh bread from his hands, cry with gratitude at his feet, and feast at his banquet. You'll bow your head, look into a reflection pool, and see heaven opened to you. You'll want to share this experience with your friends.

Bill AND Kristi Gaultiere, founders and leaders of Soul Shepherding (retreats and training in spiritual direction) and authors of *Journey of the Soul*

We all know we should spend time in the wisdom of the parables; what we don't always know is how to engage with these monumental teachings. Paired with the earthy approach of *The Message*, this thoughtful, invitational guide leads us into imaginative spaces to linger, discovering new treasures in familiar places. What a wonderful gift!

Nathan Foster, host of *Life with God: A Renovaré Podcast* and author of *The Making of an Ordinary Saint*

What makes this book truly rare is its invitation: not merely to learn but also to listen. To respond. To encounter. Within these pages is a simple yet sacred rhythm that can move you from knowing about God to communing with him. These ancient stories, both timely and timeless, are meant not just to be understood but to be lived. Be warned: This is not a passive read. If you let it, this book will draw you into a deeper, more personal engagement with God. Open wide the doors of your soul—you're being invited in.

Mindy Caliguire, founder of Soul Care and author of *Ignite Your Soul*

A 40-Day Devotional Journey in Word and Image

• • • • • • • •

PRAYING THE PARABLES OF JESUS

STEPHEN A. MACCHIA & S. K. SKINNER

FOREWORD BY ERIC E. PETERSON

NavPress

Published in alliance with Tyndale House Publishers

NavPress.com

Praying the Parables of Jesus: A 40-Day Devotional Journey in Word and Image

Copyright © 2025 by Stephen A. Macchia and Susan K. Skinner. All rights reserved.

A NavPress resource published in alliance with Tyndale House Publishers

NavPress is a registered trademark of NavPress, The Navigators, Colorado Springs, CO. The NavPress logo is a trademark of NavPress, The Navigators, Colorado Springs, CO. *Tyndale* is a registered trademark of Tyndale House Ministries. Absence of ® in connection with marks of NavPress or other parties does not indicate an absence of registration of those marks.

The Team:
David Zimmerman, Publisher; Olivia Eldredge, Acquisitions Editor; Philip F. Newman, Copyeditor; Lacie Phillips, Production Assistant; Eva M. Winters, Cover Designer; Cathy Miller, Interior Designer; Sarah Ocenasek, Proofreading Coordinator

Cover and interior charcoal drawings copyright © by Suz Skinner and used with permission. All rights reserved.

Cover illustration of Scandanavian divider copyright © by Struvictory/Adobe Stock. All rights reserved.

All Scripture quotations are taken from *The Message*, copyright © 1993, 2002, 2018 by Eugene H. Peterson. Used by permission of NavPress. All rights reserved. Represented by Tyndale House Publishers.

Some of the anecdotal illustrations in this book are true to life and are included with the permission of the persons involved. All other illustrations are composites of real situations, and any resemblance to people living or dead is purely coincidental.

For information about special discounts for bulk purchases, please contact Tyndale House Publishers at csresponse@tyndale.com, or call 1-855-277-9400.

ISBN 979-8-89802-038-5

Printed in the United States of America

31	30	29	28	27	26	25
7	6	5	4	3	2	1

To Eugene Peterson

Translator of The Message *and spiritual guide to many*

• • • • • • • • •

Contents

Foreword

About five years before my parents died, I called a family meeting that included my sister, Karen, and my brother, Leif. Recognizing some of the telltale signs indicative of a descent into both physical and cognitive decline, I was interested in getting Eugene's and Jan's responses to a long list of questions and potential scenarios so that we could honor their wishes if and when they could no longer make decisions for themselves. Most of it was routine stuff: Stay in the house or move to a retirement center? Resuscitate or DNR? Cremation or burial? Things like that.

At one point I posed a particular question directly to Eugene: "How do you want us to think about your legacy?" After his typical thoughtful pause he said, "You know, until you asked the question, I had never given it any consideration." That sounding like the final word on the topic, I went on to the next item on my list.

The following morning, as we were shuffling around the kitchen getting breakfast ready, Eugene turned to me and said, "You know, I was thinking about that legacy question, and I have an answer for you." Immediately I reached for my legal pad, preparing to capture whatever he would speak next. Looking me directly in the eyes, he said, "Eric, *you're* my legacy!"

My recollection of the moment is that we didn't discuss it any further because we didn't need to. Without saying another word, we both knew that having a share in Eugene Peterson's legacy did not mean imitating the man. Which is to say, it didn't mean running the Boston Marathon, or pastoring one church for twenty-nine years, or writing a bunch of books, or translating the Bible. Rather, it meant being *me*: the person God created me to be. That's how the son honors the father, through a legacy of faithfulness.

It's equally true in our relationships with the triune God: While we are each created in the image of God, the best way we can honor the Father is by being the unique individuals he made us to be. The ongoing legacy of Christ is manifested in the great cloud of people-witnesses who have been animated by his Spirit. This life of discipleship, however, is anything but intuitive. Much of the time it feels unnatural. Therefore, we need guidance. As usual, Jesus leads the way. As usual, it's a circuitous way.

Jesus was and is a master in the art of intrigue. The indirect ways he often spoke left his listeners alternately offended or delighted, but never disinterested. He was impossible to ignore or dismiss. Such is the power of human curiosity.

Recent studies in neuroscience have revealed the human brain's affinity for stories. In addition to hooking our attention, the best ones invite participation; they make room for us to find *ourselves* in the story. This is how Jesus created us: hardwired for stories. Storytelling, as a result, was his favored pedagogy. His parables, in particular, reflect (actually, they *anticipate*) Emily Dickinson's poetic wisdom to "tell all the truth but tell it slant."[1]

When it comes to our spiritual formation, twenty-first century North American culture makes for a poor educational classroom, permeated as it is with the capital-istic values of acquisition, consumption, and production. But the parables turn those values on their head as they champion the almost laughable values of being least, last, little, and lost. For those who have ears that hear and eyes that see, the parables lead modern-day disciples to the trailhead of liberation: pointing us down the path that releases us from slavery into the freedom of God's capacious Kingdom.

As we read the parables of Jesus on their own terms, our worldview is reshaped from one that is oriented around the value systems of the empire to the unique and sometimes-offensive ways of the Kingdom. Accordingly, if we're not squirming a little, we're probably not reading them properly. They are designed, I am persuaded, to be compelling, perplexing, even corrective. That's why we keep coming back to them; they are an endless source of invitations to take yet another step closer to God.

As a pastor, my great hope, for myself and for others—to become fit for citizenship in the Kingdom of Heaven—is accompanied by my great trust in the Scriptures to reveal the distinct ways of God. The parables of Jesus are among the most effective of biblical genres for doing exactly that. But like with anything that is old and familiar, their potency can become diminished over time. New translations, accompanied by various art forms and other creative interpretations, are needed in each generation to convey fresh invitations to the Way and the Truth of abundant Life to a world full of hungry hearts that often have misplaced affections and misdirected appetites.

Consequently, I'm always on the lookout for ungimmicky, trustworthy resources to lead people into a deepening intimacy with the Lover of our souls. In *Praying the Parables of Jesus*, S. K. Skinner and Steve Macchia have given us just such a gift, resulting in a beautiful example of Eugene's legacy.

Allow me to come in through the back door to share an idea I've been working on: The pastoral vocation, charging me with the care and the cure of souls, has deepened my appreciation for the sacraments. Over the years, I have come to see that baptism and communion (you could add up to another five, depending on your tradition) serve as a way to sanctify our sensibilities so that we grow to experience the divine presence everywhere. That Jesus chose such common elements as water, bread, and wine to be the tangible signs of our new life in him alerts us to the sacred presence that is all around us in the ordinariness of our days.

In other words, we don't have to be confined to a church or be located around a table or font to experience all life sacramentally. The Kingdom is pervasive in our world (consider the yeast) and there is, therefore, much to taste and see, to smell and hear and touch, to know that God is with us.

Similarly, I am persuaded that Jesus didn't exhaust all the possible images to describe the uniqueness of our new life as citizens of his Kingdom. He reached for the ones at hand to stimulate and to sanctify our imaginations, but that was just to prime the sensory pump. There are endless objects and experiences in this moment in church history that can be used as signs to awaken a sleepy world to the reality of God. And because everything about the gospel is livable, we ourselves ultimately become incarnate parables that enact the Good News and point people to the way of Jesus. Perhaps the genius of the parables is in their imprecision ("God's kingdom is *like*"): They leave lots of room for us to enter them as participants and to give others a glimpse of what the Kingdom's like.

I welcomed a new visitor to worship recently. She described an on-again, (mostly) off-again spiritual life that was as eclectic as the tattoos that adorned her arms. But with the birth of her daughter ("a little child shall lead them"), she was motivated to figure out what she believed. When she asked me for a recommendation of what to read in order to understand the uniqueness of the Christian faith, and to determine if it was right for her and her children, I'm embarrassed to admit that I didn't have a ready answer for her; I could not come up with a title or a resource that would simultaneously inform her head and delight her heart in a way that introduced her to the Lover of her soul.

I hope she comes back soon, because now I do. As sure as it is in your hands, you can be assured that I will put it into hers.

Eric Eugene Peterson
Colbert Presbyterian Church

Welcome

Thank you for joining us on a unique prayer journey through the parables of Jesus.

With stunning simplicity, our Lord taught about the Kingdom of Heaven through the medium of stories. Each with a unique richness and vitality, the parables have stood the test of time and continue to resonate with disciples of every generation. In many respects, they are stories that never end—always there for us to receive as a fresh gift from God.

Both of us, from our particular backgrounds, have benefited significantly from Jesus' clarion call through the parables to be fully abandoned to Kingdom priorities. They are, of course, merely one slice of the beautiful and robust kaleidoscope of prayer offered to us as dearly loved children of God. But in our ministries of spiritual direction and companionship, praying the parables has helped us, together with those we guide, experience richer and fuller lives with God.

We have constructed this prayer resource around the ancient practices of lectio divina and visio divina. Through these practices God uses both word and image to enhance our ability to hear and see the Word coming to life in our hearts. We invite you to enter this space with creative anticipation and prayerful delight.

Take it slow.
Savor deeply.
Notice the invitations of the Spirit.

Pray.
Listen.
Apply.
Integrate.
Notice.
Love.

For this book we are using the parables as rendered in *The Message*, Eugene Peterson's paraphrase of the Scriptures. But we also encourage you to read the parables from your favorite Bible translation alongside these exercises. We are convinced that doing so will enhance your prayerful experience.

Our number one hope is that this journey of praying the parables will deepen your intimacy with Jesus, the Author of these life-changing stories, and your own ever-unfolding, life-transforming story of faith and God's faithfulness.

Our prayers are yours as you venture forth into the parables of Jesus. Engage your whole heart, soul, mind, and strength into all that awaits you. God bless you and keep you; may his face shine upon you and be gracious to you.

Let us know how it goes for you.

Your friends in prayer,
Suz Skinner and Steve Macchia

Introduction

Praying It Slant

. . . .

A mustard seed. A lampstand. Weeds. Yeast. A pearl. Two sons. A fruit tree. Talents. Sheep and goats. A good Samaritan. A rich fool. A lost coin. A lost son. A persistent widow.

These are just some of the stories Jesus loved to tell—stories we love to hear. His rationale for the parables is pretty straightforward: "I tell stories," he says in Matthew 13:13, "to create readiness, to nudge the people toward a welcome awakening."

Jesus recognizes, of course, that a nudge is no guarantee that someone will wake up:

"You've been given insight into God's kingdom. You know how it works. Not everybody has this gift, this insight; it hasn't been given to them. Whenever someone has a ready heart for this, the insights and understandings flow freely. But if there is no readiness, any trace of receptivity soon disappears. . . . In their present state they can stare till doomsday and not see it, listen till they're blue in the face and not get it. I don't want Isaiah's forecast repeated all over again:

Your ears are open but you don't hear a thing.
    Your eyes are awake but you don't see a thing.
The people are stupid!
They stick their fingers in their ears
    so they won't have to listen;

They screw their eyes shut
>   so they won't have to look,
>   so they won't have to deal with me face-to-face
>   and let me heal them.

"But you have God-blessed eyes—eyes that see! And God-blessed ears—
ears that hear!"

MATTHEW 13:11-16

How about you? Do you have eyes that see and ears that hear? We live in a time that is thick with information; we are weighed down by its heaviness. We have every definition, explanation, and perception on any subject, large or small, promptly available to us. We are patterned to encounter life through efficient, instantly gratifying means. We are impatient in our approach to life.

In an instant age, have we lost the capacity to wait? Even our prayer lives are vulnerable to the allure of instantaneous clarity. We come to God with lists, expectations, and requests, leaving little room for deep relationship, attentive listening, enhanced trust.

In such an environment, what are we missing? What significant insights might only be revealed slowly, gradually? What important decisions are being made haphazardly? Might our conversations, our relationships, be irreducibly complex?

Our age may be built around efficiency, but we were created to, as Eugene Peterson puts it, savor subtleties and relish ambiguities.[2] We were designed to be attentive, to be patient, to ponder. Like poems, or paintings, or beautiful sunsets, Jesus' parables honor this design. His stories are a way to "tell all the truth," as Emily Dickinson writes, "but tell it slant."[3]

Jesus' parables suggest that God desires to reveal himself, impart wisdom, and bestow gifts on his children in a way that cultivates with and within us "unhurried intimacies."[4] The Scriptures assure us that one day we will "see it all as clearly as God sees us, knowing him directly just as he knows us" (1 Corinthians 13:12). But maybe for now, our encounters with God in prayer are meant to take place in what seems like a fog or a mist as we let our affections for him and our trust in him increase.

Tilted Heads, Spinning Hearts

The parables of Jesus make our heads tilt with wonder and our hearts spin with curiosity.

We listen to each story and are arrested by the profundity of its message. One after another, each simple parable offers life change to the hearer. It points us toward the priorities of the Kingdom of Heaven and persistently invites us to embrace the way of Jesus.

It's really that straightforward, and yet the parables are consistently delivered by Jesus with titillating and unnerving obliqueness. We listen and are left tongue-tied for a moment. If we have eyes that see and ears that hear, then slowly and reflectively, with curiosity and awe, we begin to prayerfully wonder how best to respond.

In his book *Tell It Slant*, Eugene Peterson suggests that the parables are Jesus' primary means for teaching about the Kingdom of Heaven:

The parable . . . is a way of saying something that requires the imaginative participation of the listener. Inconspicuously, even surreptitiously, a parable *involves* the hearer. This brief, commonplace, unpretentious story is thrown into a conversation and lands at our feet, compelling notice. A parable is literally "something thrown alongside of" (*para*, alongside, plus *bolē*, thrown) to which our first response is, "What is *this* doing here?" We ask questions, we think, we imagine. . . . And then we begin seeing connections, relations. A parable is not ordinarily used to tell us something new but to get us to notice something that we have overlooked. . . . Or it is used to get us to take seriously something we have dismissed as unimportant because we have never seen the point of it. Before we know it, we are involved. . . .

A parable comes up on the listener obliquely, on the "slant."[5]

Jesus' message of the Kingdom of Heaven is consistent; conveyed with poignancy and grace; employing imagination, creativity, and invitation. His parables are captivating and powerful, winsome and life altering. Never too complex, always simple, direct, meaningful, relevant, and powerful. Never in a hurry, and with an uncanny economy of words, Jesus expresses God's heart for the lost, the least, the lonely, the little, and the left behind. And he welcomes them home with wide-open arms.

While only some of the parables end with a cliff-hanger, we consistently find ourselves on the edge of the cliff, with a necessary, consequential next step in front of us. Each parable elicits a response. Choose today the Kingdom of Heaven, and all other things will be added unto you.

The parables are both the ends and the means of Jesus' truth telling. Their invitations to reorder our lives according to Kingdom priorities are gentle and piercing, filled with grace, truth, justice, and mercy. Guided by and toward God's loving truth, the parables (with the head-scratching manner of communication found in them) lead us into depth of insight and radical application.

A Liberated Lifestyle of Delightful Obedience

The cost of discipleship is steep, but it is designed to set us free. Jesus was sent by the Father in the power of the Spirit to live among us, invite us into his Kingdom, suffer on our behalf, and ultimately overcome death (on the cross) and be raised gloriously, miraculously, and triumphantly as our long-awaited Messiah. His teachings—challenging to the religious elite, comforting to everyday people with ears that hear—liberate his followers toward a lifestyle of delightful obedience to a better way of living: not arbitrary rules and regulations shaped by the patterns of the world but the cruciform way of humility, servanthood, love, and compassion.

The parables are a beautiful window into the dailiness of Jesus' life, lived among his generation and emulated, embodied, and empowered through his stories.

As we read the Gospels, we see Jesus embody prayerfulness in all his interactions. He invites his disciples to listen and pray, to watch and pray. He teaches them to pray:

"The world is full of so-called prayer warriors who are prayer-ignorant. They're full of formulas and programs and advice, peddling techniques for getting what you want from God. Don't fall for that nonsense. This is your Father you are dealing with, and he knows better than you what you need. With a God like this loving you, you can pray very simply."
MATTHEW 6:7-9

In this book we invite you to pray the parables of Jesus. These stories have been preserved for us to reflect upon and to inform our way of being in our generation. As we hold Jesus' stories in quiet stillness, listening for his Spirit to illuminate them and weave them into our own stories, their truths shape our thinking, transform our living, and inform our engagement with others. We become Christlike, Kingdom-ready, Good-News people.

Starting in the Scriptures

Today there is a clarion call toward a necessary adjustment in our spiritual lives: to return to the biblical text as the primary informer of our hearts and souls, our minds and our lives. Each time the Scriptures are heard, read, and received, the Word of God comes alive. The Scriptures inform our prayers as we seek to emulate the truth of God's Word in our daily lives.

We can easily forget, in the face of many distractions, that the Scriptures were given to us as a gift to treasure, an unparalleled source of strength, the delivery system for our training in Christlike prayerfulness. When we sit with the Word, we allow it to master us rather than seeking to master it. The Bible is no dead text; it is alive with meaning and purpose and life-changing value. For you and us. Today and every day.

Making Your Way Through

We begin in the Gospel of Matthew (with parallel passages provided). One parable that appears only in the Gospel of Mark will follow, and then we will conclude with parables from the Gospel of Luke. As we do so, we are convinced that we will become ever more prayer-full in our daily lives. You will notice that the Gospel of John is not included here. Very simply, John was more concerned about presenting Jesus in expanded and explained metaphor. The parables are therefore found only in the synoptic Gospels.

We will initially consider each parable with some contextual noticings:

- The opening paragraph will offer a summary of the parable and relevant context: Where is Jesus when he's teaching the parable, and how is Jesus sensitive to the person(s) he's teaching?

- A *simile* to the Kingdom ("like"/"as") will consider how Jesus is sowing seed into the soil of our souls via a readily understandable comparison.

- *Contrast(s)* will be presented between Kingdom mindedness and worldliness: How is Jesus safeguarding the secrets of God?

As you reflect on the parable via lectio divina and visio divina, you will also notice Jesus highlighting conclusively the sovereignty and superiority of God. And you will see Jesus consistently and continuously teaching about the salvation and eternal life made possible exclusively by God. These are the big ideas of Jesus' parables, and they are unearthed as we reflect on his teachings and pray into our best response.

As we move into the passage at hand, our chosen translation of the Bible is *The Message*, Eugene Peterson's paraphrase of the Scriptures into contemporary English. Eugene is one of our spiritual heroes. We greatly appreciate his desire to make the ancient Word of God widely accessible to the modern ear and his firm commitment to accurately represent the original text. A gifted linguist with the enthusiastic support of twenty biblical scholars who reviewed his work, Peterson sought to bring the language of the Bible into the language of today. We celebrate his work.

We encourage you to read the parables with another translation of your choice, alongside *The Message*, as you pray your way through the parables. Invite the Spirit of God into the deepest recesses of your soul as your teacher and trailblazer, comforter and guide.

Our invitation as you read each parable is as follows:

- Engage with the parables prayerfully, expectantly, and joyfully.

- Tilt your head with eager curiosity. Enter the scene of each parable and absorb the storyline and eternal meaning of the passage. Then stay alert to what God has for you on this day.

- Instead of reading with your mind alone, exercise your creativity and let your heart feel the deeper meaning of the texts at hand. Pray that the seeds of each parable will be planted deeply in your heart and soul.

- Take it slow. Don't turn the page until you've had a relationally engaging experience with Jesus. Use this as an opportunity to cultivate unhurried intimacy with your Messiah, King, Savior, and Lord.

You'll be helped in this process by the two ancient practices of lectio divina and visio divina.

Lectio divina (which means "sacred reading") was the primary way the Scriptures were historically prayed within religious monastic communities. It was a practice that Benedict of Nursia established in the sixth century to help people imaginatively enter into and meet God in a Bible passage. It was the belief of the early church fathers and mothers that the biblical text was central to one's life of faith. To absorb the Word of God into the mind, heart, and soul of the listener was the primary means of building up and strengthening the church. As Eugene Peterson describes it,

> *Lectio divina* is the deliberate and intentional practice of . . . listening to, accompanying, and following Jesus alive. . . . It is not just a skill that we exercise when we have a Bible open before us but a life congruent with the Word made flesh to which the Scriptures give witness.[6]

The spiritual discipline of lectio divina has been a principal means for generations of Christians to experience a divine encounter with God through the pages of the Bible. As Eugene Peterson writes in his introduction to *The Message*, "The Bible is not only written about us but to us. In these pages we become insiders to a conversation in which God uses words to form and bless us, to teach and guide us, to forgive and save us."[7] Slowly and prayerfully engaging with the Scriptures, we will follow the ancient intervals of reading and praying:

- stopping and resting for a moment and preparing to encounter God in the Bible (*silencio* is the Latin term; *pause* is the modern word we will use);

- doing a first reading and then making observations about the scriptural text (*lectio* or *read*);

- reflecting on what we observe in our reading of the text a second time and in ourselves as we read and notice (*meditatio* or *ponder*);

- engaging in conversation with God inspired by the text (*oratio* or *pray*) after reading the text another time and noting the prayer that's evoked;

- taking note of what this time with God has brought to the surface (*contemplatio* or *reflect*), even as we prayerfully reflect on the text one more time; and, finally,

- considering how this time with God translates into our lives with God (*incarnatio* or *live*) and choosing responsively how best to live out the text we've prayed. God may also be simply inviting us to rest in his grace and receive the parable as a gift for our souls.[8]

Another way to consider lectio divina is simply to acknowledge the powerful impact of a repetitive read of the same passage of Scripture—slowly, perhaps audibly, repeating the words over and over again, letting them wash over and deeply embed themselves into the fibers of our minds, hearts, and souls.

There is a resurgence of interest in and fascination with the use of lectio divina today—an excellent sign of spiritual renewal and one that we affirm and encourage, particularly in this text.

Visio divina is a complementary practice to lectio divina. Although *visio divina* is a relatively recent term, Christians have been contemplating God through art and nature for millennia. Early Christians painted Bible scenes in catacombs. In the Middle Ages, stained-glass cathedral windows and illuminated Bible manuscripts helped worshipers experience God in nonverbal ways. As we see in Greek and Russian Orthodox churches around the globe, venerating icons has been and is today an important way Orthodox Christians pray.

Visio divina uses images instead of words to heighten one's attentiveness to the meaning of the passage. To see in this context will include gazing, looking, observing, noticing—all the ways we see with our internal heart and mind's eye. Just as lectio divina invites people to meditate on Scripture, visio divina helps people pray with art. *Visio divina* translates as "divine seeing," and the practice uses silence and images to help worshipers reflect and respond to God in ways other than listening to sermons or singing praise songs.

Since there's no single correct way to practice visio divina, there's room to improvise. Whether alone or in a group, people tend to focus on a single work of art, often with a biblical or religious theme. You can also pray with your eyes while admiring a garden, walking along the ocean, hiking a mountain, or even spending time in an urban neighborhood. Some visio divina experiences include guided prompts and time to share insights.[9]

As you ponder and pray with the graphite drawings for each parable, and with their corresponding prompts for reflection, we hope that the artwork's "tell it slant" nature will be yet another invitation to pray it slant with the parables. We follow the same sixfold process noted above, but instead of reading the text, we engage with a visual representation of Jesus' imagery-rich storytelling (a uniquely designed image created by coauthor and artist S. K. Skinner) through questions for reflection and prayer.

It's important to note that even though we are presenting the sixfold nature of lectio and visio divina in their traditional linear progression, we invite freedom and joy in their use. The more you become familiar with lectio and visio divina, the more you will encounter the Spirit's often mysterious, creative, and surprising leading. We believe that to hold the process openhandedly is to remain openhearted. Let's not become rigid like the Pharisees of old; instead, let's remain agile and fluid and flexible, open to the continual move of the Spirit in, through, among, and all around us as eager disciples of Jesus.

Lectio and visio divina are all about praying the Word and, as the Word comes alive, participating in the Spirit's prompting to live the Word. As we are led by the Spirit, our belief will lead to our action. We hope that these practices, creatively accompanied by word and beauty, will be instilled into your ongoing life of prayer. Slow down. Listen. Receive. Reflect. Obey. Remain open to the Spirit as you read, notice, and pray. This posture will lead you to the heart of God and to Kingdom-focused righteousness and faithfulness.

A Note on the Parable of the Prodigal Son and the Older Son

This parable, told in Luke 15:11-32, is long and multifaceted. To give due consideration to the complexity of the parable, we've divided it into two parts ("35a: The Prodigal Son" and "35b: The Older Son"). You are free to go through both these sections in one sitting or spread them out over two. (Doing the latter would make this a forty-one-day journey through forty parables.)

Guidance for Group Use

In hopes of our readers using this material in their own personal prayer closets as well as with small groups, we offer the following guidance for group use. However, simply gathering with a group of peers who desire to go deep into the parables and share from their personal prayer experiences is terrific. A suggested basic overview for such a gathering looks like this:

1. Choose a time that works for everyone, perhaps weekly or biweekly. Commit to coming prepared to each gathering, working through a previously designated number of parables prior to arrival.

2. Begin your time together with casual fellowship and a simple form of welcome. Practice tangible hospitality before sitting together in a circle, then offer a time to be silent together in community before leading in prayer.

3. Invite everyone to offer personal reflections about their encounter with the designated parable(s). How did their lectio and/or visio divina experience deepen their understanding and application of the biblical text? Most importantly, how did the parable(s) deepen their intimacy with Jesus?

4. Try not to interrupt as each person shares from the heart. Listen as best as possible from the soul level. Only comment about what you heard if invited to do so, and then simply provide a verbatim of what you heard. Don't attempt to fix theology you disagree with, compare or contrast someone's story with yours, or compete with one another's insights. Simply be present with one another and practice pure listening.

5. Take your time between sharing. Perhaps invite a minute or two of silence after each person's reflections. Slow down and be loving, supportive, empathetic, compassionate, and present. Treat one another's sharing as a sacred trust offered and received in love.

6. After everyone has had the opportunity to share about their experience, invite prayers for one another as you continue to pray it slant in the coming days. Determine the next time to meet, and continue onward with this shared experience.

7. To reiterate the second item above, practice hospitality—both tangibly and intangibly—for all who come and offer themselves in this prayer experience. Don't be rushed even as the time comes to an end. Leisurely release and bless one another as you depart.

Notice how praying the parables transforms your personal time with the Lord in your prayer closet. Talk with your spiritual companions about your experience. Combine your individual experiences with community, and watch how your friendships in Christ are enhanced. We trust that by practicing the traditional phases of lectio divina as you pray the parables of Jesus you will incorporate this way of praying the Scriptures hereafter. Although the visio divina questions will be unique for each parable (while following the ancient order), the lectio divina queries will remain consistent for the sake of learning this form of prayer repetitively: silencio/pause, lectio/read, meditatio/ponder, oratio/pray, contemplatio/reflect, and incarnatio/live. We pray that the Word of God will come alive in your heart and soul with each and every prayerful consideration of the parables of Jesus.

A story-rich prayer life awaits you.

Frequently Asked Questions
about the Parables of Jesus

Why did Jesus teach in parables?

Jesus' desire was to cultivate an *unhurried intimacy* with every person he met. The use of stories and real-life illustrations connected each hearer with his heart, the truthful message to a simple story. From Eugene Peterson:

> The people we meet "on the road" and "between Sundays" expect to deal with things on their own terms, meanwhile keeping God in his place where he belongs. . . .
>
> Parables are [Jesus'] primary language of choice. . . . As the stakes increase, his language becomes even more relaxed and conversational than usual. Instead of high decibel rhetoric, calling for decisions before it is too late, he hardly, if at all, even mentions the name of God, choosing instead to speak of neighbors and friends, losing a lamb, and the courtesies of hospitality.[10]

Jesus spoke in parables in fulfillment of what had been spoken by the prophets: "I will open my mouth and tell stories; I will bring out into the open things hidden since the world's first day" (Matthew 13:35, referencing Psalm 78:2). Jesus knew his underlying focus for living among, with, and for the people—to point them toward the Kingdom of God—and he kept that focus throughout his three years of radical teaching. But he always kept the truth accessible to each soul within earshot. Each parable was unique to the moment and circumstance, highlighting one important truth.

We tend to forget that Jesus was a teacher and not a writer, although what we know of him was written down by his followers and (thankfully) preserved for our knowledge, transformation, and ongoing reflection. His was an oral culture; beyond the sacred Scriptures, very little teaching was communicated by writing.

Whom did Jesus hope to reach with the parables?

Jesus' teaching generally took place in open, public spaces, allowing him to bypass the institutionalized religious authorities and speak directly to a broad swath of everyday people. By and large, his parables involved scenarios quickly relatable to a working-class audience. "They were surprised and impressed" by his "forthright" teaching style, "not the quibbling and quoting they were used to" (Luke 4:32). In many ways, the parables were for people hungry and thirsty for righteousness and were rather hidden from the self-righteous or self-satisfied, who were too smug to learn from such simple teaching.

The religious authorities were regularly present in these crowds, and some of Jesus' parables were addressed to them directly. Their response to these parables was generally frustration and resistance, although some certainly moved toward Jesus and not away from him. Recall Jesus' rationale for teaching in parables from Matthew 13:13, 15: "That's why I tell stories: to create readiness. . . . [But some] people are stupid! They stick their fingers in their ears so they won't have to listen; they screw their eyes shut so they won't have to look, so they won't have to deal with me face-to-face and let me heal them."

What do the parables do for us today?

The parables offer us a blueprint for paying attention to the world around us while also pointing us to the heart of God and the Kingdom of Heaven. Like the burning bush that God used to capture Moses' attention, the parables elicit our curiosity in order to draw us into the majesty and dominion of Jesus, where we hear his call to a life of Kingdom service.

The parables are both story and prayer, moving straight out of everyday life into the inner sanctuaries of our souls. Parables breed both faithfulness and fruitfulness, for they point to the way of Jesus for all to follow.

How did Jesus construct each parable?

Although we see no evidence of Jesus taking time to craft his parables, we do see several traits in common among them. Each parable seems to flow naturally, lovingly, and prayerfully from his heart. Each is timely for the particular incident and relationship. Here are some common traits of the parables:

- *Simplicity.* Each parable is brief and easy to understand. The parables are poignant, connected to real-life experiences.

- *Clarity.* Each parable has a distinct message to proclaim. They are always spoken in love, designed to liberate the hearers.

- *Meaning.* Each parable alludes to the Kingdom of Heaven. This Kingdom is both present and future, and it includes here-and-now priorities such as discipleship, prayer, money and wealth, limitless grace, forgiveness, justice, mercy, and righteousness.

- *Contrast.* Each parable presents a stark contrast. In every story there is a binary choice to be made: to seek or reject life in God's Kingdom.

- *The ability to stand alone.* Each parable is spoken in the moment. Even where parables show up in groups and share similarities (for example, the parables in Luke 15 that focus on the lost sheep, the lost coin, and the lost son), each parable is designed to confront a particular problem and force a specific choice.

- *Invitation.* Each parable is an encouragement to deeper holiness. The parables are offered to fortify faith, increase understanding, and foster obedience to the Father, Son, and Holy Spirit.

- *Freedom.* Each parable is designed to teach faithfulness and righteousness. Jesus' teaching on these subjects is liberating in its contrast to the regulations and rigidity of the dominant religious teaching of the day.

What did Jesus hope to evoke in the hearts of his hearers?

Each of the parables highlights eternal truth and illuminates the path forward for the open and receptive disciple. And they have evoked responses, both in the hearts of the hearers and in the lives of the ones who have both ears that can hear and the desire to choose rightly. One cannot help but pause, meditate (even for a moment), and then decide what to do in response. Jesus walks all the way to the edge and is there to hold our hands as we trust him to carry us forward.

When did Jesus desire a response to the parables?

The parables range in size from a single verse to a longer and more detailed story. Of course, faithfulness was his desired outcome. However, the jarring nature of the choices offered would challenge many, especially given the confrontation of thought presented.

In his parables, Jesus encouraged people to stop, look, and listen—to experience new insight, to let their consciences be stirred, to consider the appropriate response. To say yes to Jesus is to say no to any number of consequential alternatives. To follow Jesus is radical to say the least.

Where is the context for each story?

The beauty of the parables is that each one is unique to the context into which Jesus spoke. That's why we don't see him justifying his approach or having a canned response everywhere he traveled. That fact alone should elicit praise and awe in our hearts as readers and bystanders to the teachable moment each parable offered then and offers now.

The overall purpose of each parable is to invite immediate and obedient response to the invitation to follow Jesus and abide by his Kingdom-centered righteousness. But, with spontaneity and creativity, we are given a glimpse into the heart of Jesus by attending to the very words he uses and the stories he conveys. All his presentations are masterful.

What is the Kingdom Jesus talks about in the parables?

Jesus, the second person of the Trinity, came to earth to establish a Kingdom focused on heaven. The eternality of the Kingdom Jesus proclaimed is also evoked in the prophetic message of the Old Testament; it is echoed and embodied in the New Testament writings and the apostolic age of the early church.

The Kingdom of Heaven (also known as the Kingdom of God) is an already/not-yet Kingdom of what was, what is, and what remains ahead of us. For disciples who follow King Jesus, our interior life and our outward expressions of allegiance are meant to reflect the purposes and priorities he carries and communicates. God's Word helps us understand and live into this focus. Our submission to God's will and way is how we promote the Kingdom of God, proclaimed by Christ.

Why are the parables only in the Synoptics (Matthew, Mark, and Luke) and not in the Gospel of John?

Matthew uses brevity to convey the parables of Jesus, much like a tax collector would be economical in his use of words. Luke, on the other hand, tends toward a greater amount of color commentary about the life and personalities involved. Only a couple of parables are unique to Mark's Gospel. One is "The Growing Seed" (Mark 4:26-29). Another is "The Absent Homeowner" (Mark 13:32-37), which we have combined with Luke 12:35-40, "The Watchful Servants," a close parallel text.

In contrast, the Gospel of John highlights Jesus' use of metaphor. For example, Jesus uses the seven "I am" statements: "I am the Bread of Life" (John 6:35), "I am the world's Light" (John 8:12), "I am the Gate" (John 10:7), "I am the Good Shepherd" (John 10:11, 14), "I am . . . Resurrection and Life" (John 11:25), "I am the Road, also the Truth, also the Life" (John 14:6), and "I am the Real Vine" (John 15:1). Throughout the Gospel of John, we see major portraits of Jesus unveiled in each chapter, pointing specifically to the unique roles Jesus fulfills (such as Son of God, Son of Man, divine teacher, etc.). These themes are considered in Steve Macchia's book *Path of a Beloved Disciple: 31 Days in the Gospel of John*.[11]

What in particular should I pay attention to in the artwork?

To pray it slant, we must not be too polished, too complete, or too overstated. We must leave room for what is yet to be imagined or discovered. Graphite pencil is a medium that is particularly conducive to this approach.

Playfully, like a good pun, most of these compositions were built upon an oblique angle (a real concept in geometry). Some of these angles are subtle, others are in-your-face on purpose. In the world of design, angles and diagonal lines are used to create depth and perspective. Also, diagonals depict movement or action. A design based upon a triangle creates compositional strength in the same way a three-legged stool is quite steady. Or sometimes a diagonal line is meant to cause a disturbance or delineation. See if you can find the oblique angles in each drawing.

In addition, there are hidden treasures that may require an intentional search (even research). A Hebrew word, a seeing eye, feathered wings, a halo-like crown, the ninety-nine, the presence of angels, an acorn, poison darnel—what hidden treasures will you find?

Not merely illustrations, these drawings are meant to cause us to wonder just beyond the obvious, to discover something new or something more. Stay with the ones that capture your imagination. Allow God to meet you in what is not always clear or familiar. Permit the artwork to slow you down, and let yourself linger there with Jesus in your place of prayer.

To learn about the background behind each piece of art, visit Suz Skinner's website:

I

THE LAMP ON A STAND

Matthew 5:14-16; Mark 4:21-22; Luke 8:16-18; 11:33-36

. . . .

In the Sermon on the Mount, speaking to a great crowd, Jesus describes how his followers are to make the way of God known. It's never to be hidden or withheld. For the eager hearer, especially one inclined toward the voice of Jesus, this message offers comfort and courage, conviction and hope. Go public. No secrets. Let your light shine.

SIMILE. Lamps are created to be lit, dispelling the darkness that engulfs daily life. They are to be not only ignited but also free of distraction or obstruction. Anyone who considers hiding a light, keeping it under a bucket or hidden under a table, isn't using it correctly. Our lives, fashioned around Jesus' life, are to brightly illuminate the path so that all may see.

CONTRAST. The light of a well-lit lamp consumes the darkness that surrounds it. Light and life go hand in glove, as do darkness and death. The contrast between light and darkness is palpable, and a covered-over lamp withholds the light from shining forth as it's meant to. The truth of the Kingdom life of God is to be shining brightly for all to see.

LECTIO DIVINA

PAUSE. Sit silently and reverently with the Lord and invite him to make his presence known to you during this prayerfully reflective experience.

READ. Read the parable of Jesus a few times, either silently or aloud. Begin to notice what words and/or phrases pop off the page and land in your heart.

PONDER. Meditate on the parable, lingering with each word on the page. Note what's being formed in your heart and mind around the meaning of the parable.

PRAY. Formulate a prayer based on what you're noticing in the parable. Pay particular attention to the prompting of the Spirit toward one aspect of the parable.

REFLECT. Hold the parable like a diamond or a prism, looking at it from as many angles as possible. Notice any nuance or texture to the parable that feels invitational.

LIVE. Incarnate the truth you've discovered for your life today. Ask the Lord if there is one aspect of today's parable that you need to emulate in your sphere of influence. Or simply receive the parable as a gift for your soul.

THE LAMP ON A STAND

Matthew 5:14-16

"Here's another way to put it: You're here to be light, bringing out the God-colors in the world. God is not a secret to be kept. We're going public with this, as public as a city on a hill. If I make you light-bearers, you don't think I'm going to hide you under a bucket, do you? I'm putting you on a light stand. Now that I've put you there on a hilltop, on a light stand— shine! Keep open house; be generous with your lives. By opening up to others, you'll prompt people to open up with God, this generous Father in heaven."

See also Mark 4:21-22; Luke 8:16-18; 11:33-36

VISIO DIVINA

PAUSE. Take a moment to ask the Lord to help you focus on what he has for you as you pray with this drawing, *Shine.*

SEE. Let your eyes travel from the foreground into the background of the drawing and back again, from light to shadows, from clarity to darkness. How do contrast and repetition in the drawing play with the themes of the parable?

PONDER. How do you imagine the movement of the bowl or the bucket? Is it being lowered or lifted? Consider what each movement reveals as light is either hidden or allowed to spill out into the open. What emotions, memories, or curiosities arise in you?

PRAY. Be still with the Lord. Talk to him about what you are noticing.

REFLECT. What self-awareness (personal thought or reaction) or God-awareness (sense of God with you) occurs in your prayer? Look at the drawing once more. Is there anything new this time?

LIVE. Consider how this parable translates into your present-day life. Do you sense an invitation from the Lord to live differently?

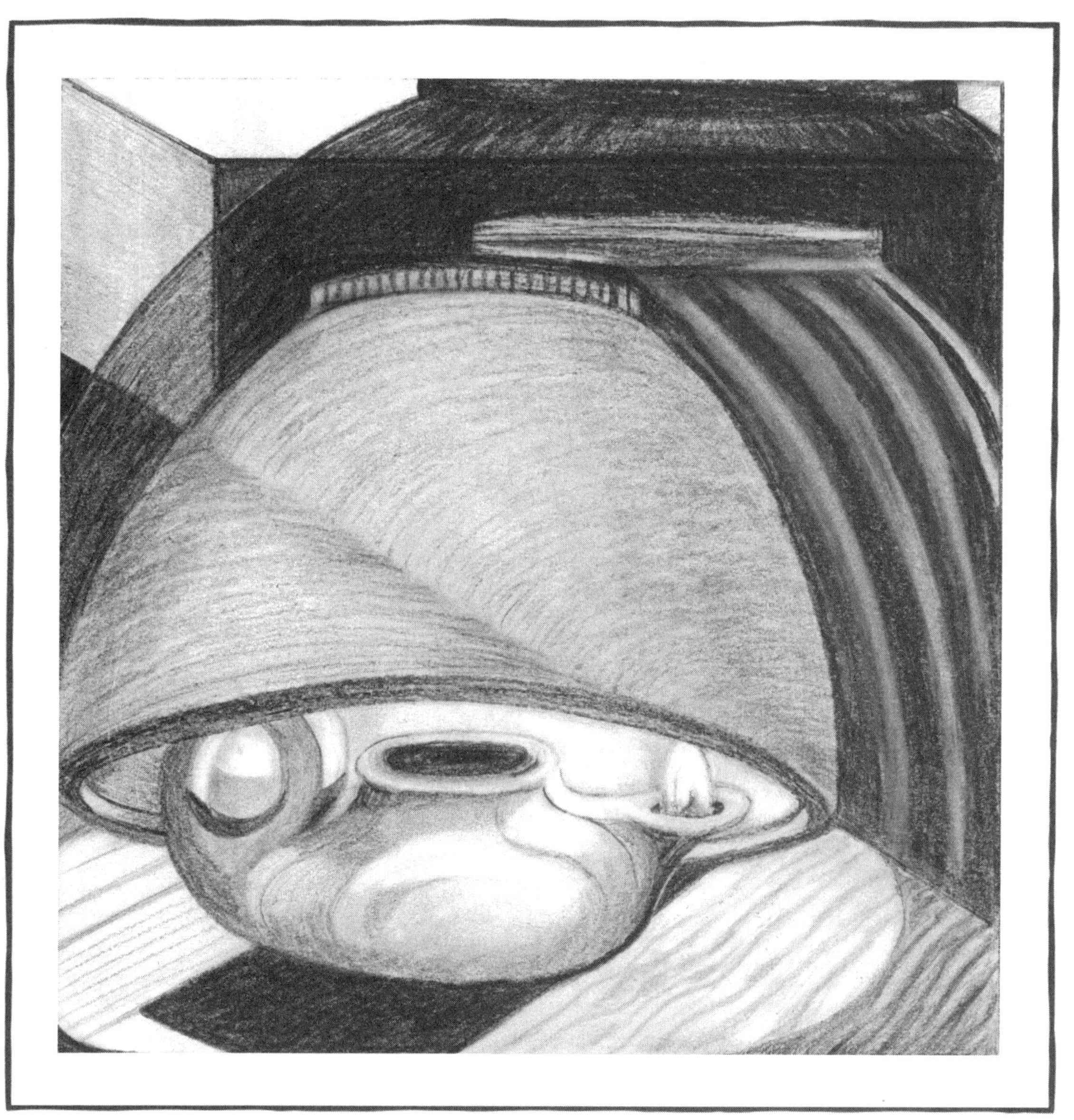

SHINE

2

THE WISE BUILDER
AND THE FOOLISH BUILDER

Matthew 7:24-27; Luke 6:46-49

. . . .

As the Sermon on the Mount is coming to conclusion, Jesus is summarizing his desired response for all who have heard his teaching. If you have ears that hear, then choose wisely and circumspectly as you build or rebuild your life in God. A firm foundation will keep one upright and secure amid the inevitable storms of life.

SIMILE. For all who choose to build their lives around Kingdom priorities, Jesus is inviting his hearers to live faithfully and fruitfully. Extolling wisdom and fortitude, he urges each one to be like a wise owner or a smart carpenter. Building life on a firm foundation will ensure a stability that only God can provide. Choosing sand rather than rock will lead to eventual collapse.

CONTRAST. Jesus makes it clear that choosing to follow his teaching is like being a wise carpenter who builds his life on a firm foundation. This stands in stark contrast to being a foolish person who follows after a lifestyle tenuously built on sand. When the inevitable storms of life blow and beat on the houses, one is left standing while the other falls with a crash and washes away.

LECTIO DIVINA

PAUSE. Sit silently and reverently with the Lord and invite him to make his presence known to you during this prayerfully reflective experience.

READ. Read the parable of Jesus a few times, either silently or aloud. Begin to notice what words and/or phrases pop off the page and land in your heart.

PONDER. Meditate on the parable, lingering with each word on the page. Note what's being formed in your heart and mind around the meaning of the parable.

PRAY. Formulate a prayer based on what you're noticing in the parable. Pay particular attention to the prompting of the Spirit toward one aspect of the parable.

REFLECT. Hold the parable like a diamond or a prism, looking at it from as many angles as possible. Notice any nuance or texture to the parable that feels invitational.

LIVE. Incarnate the truth you've discovered for your life today. Ask the Lord if there is one aspect of today's parable that you need to emulate in your sphere of influence. Or simply receive the parable as a gift for your soul.

THE WISE BUILDER AND THE FOOLISH BUILDER
Matthew 7:24-27

"These words I speak to you are not incidental additions to your life, homeowner improvements to your standard of living. They are foundational words, words to build a life on. If you work these words into your life, you are like a smart carpenter who built his house on solid rock. Rain poured down, the river flooded, a tornado hit—but nothing moved that house. It was fixed to the rock.

"But if you just use my words in Bible studies and don't work them into your life, you are like a stupid carpenter who built his house on the sandy beach. When a storm rolled in and the waves came up, it collapsed like a house of cards."

See also Luke 6:46-49

VISIO DIVINA

PAUSE. Recall what words or phrases stood out to you in the parable. Ask God to unfold more as you prayerfully look upon this drawing, *Built upon the Rock*.

SEE. What is your eye drawn to as you scan the whole scene? Remain with this image in a posture of prayerful curiosity. Notice what is evoked in the contrast that you see.

PONDER. What part of the story is left out for you to complete in your imagination?

PRAY. As you imagine and ponder the two impending outcomes of the story, what comes up for you?

REFLECT. How might considering the themes of vulnerability and security spur you on with the desire to put into practice the words of Jesus?

LIVE. What would it look like for you to hear Jesus' words and "work them into your life" (Matthew 7:26)? What next step is the Lord inviting you to take in building your life on the foundational words and ways of Jesus?

BUILT UPON THE ROCK

3

NEW CLOTH ON AN OLD GARMENT

Matthew 9:14-17; Mark 2:19-22; Luke 5:34-39

• • • • • • • •

On the heels of calling Matthew to follow him, Jesus is answering John the Baptist's disciples, who are asking him about his frequency of fasting and inconsistency with the Pharisees. This upends their first-century expectations of the Messiah building on their traditions. The old has passed away, and the new has come (see 2 Corinthians 5:17).

SIMILE. The Kingdom of Heaven is diametrically opposed to the old way of rules and regulations set forth by the Pharisees and teachers of the law. What Jesus is proclaiming in their presence is like a fine silk scarf, preferred and disassociated from the old work clothes that have become binding, restrictive, and outdated.

CONTRAST. Jesus is making it clear to his listeners that it's nonsensical to consider patching the old garment with a piece of unshrunk cloth. If that's done, it won't last long. The new piece of cloth will pull away from the old. Like a piece of unshrunk cloth, Jesus' message isn't fitting into the religious systems of the time.

LECTIO DIVINA

PAUSE. Sit silently and reverently with the Lord and invite him to make his presence known to you during this prayerfully reflective experience.

READ. Read the parable of Jesus a few times, either silently or aloud. Begin to notice what words and/or phrases pop off the page and land in your heart.

PONDER. Meditate on the parable, lingering with each word on the page. Note what's being formed in your heart and mind around the meaning of the parable.

PRAY. Formulate a prayer based on what you're noticing in the parable. Pay particular attention to the prompting of the Spirit toward one aspect of the parable.

REFLECT. Hold the parable like a diamond or a prism, looking at it from as many angles as possible. Notice any nuance or texture to the parable that feels invitational.

LIVE. Incarnate the truth you've discovered for your life today. Ask the Lord if there is one aspect of today's parable that you need to emulate in your sphere of influence. Or simply receive the parable as a gift for your soul.

NEW CLOTH ON AN OLD GARMENT

Matthew 9:14-17

A little later John's followers approached, asking, "Why is it that we and the Pharisees rigorously discipline body and spirit by fasting, but your followers don't?"

Jesus told them, "When you're celebrating a wedding, you don't skimp on the cake and wine. You feast. Later you may need to exercise moderation, but not now. No one throws cold water on a friendly bonfire. This is Kingdom Come!"

He went on, "No one cuts up a fine silk scarf to patch old work clothes; you want fabrics that match. And you don't put your wine in cracked bottles."

See also Mark 2:19-22; Luke 5:34-39

VISIO DIVINA

PAUSE. Ask the Lord for insight as you contemplate this drawing, *The Patch*.

SEE. Slow down with the details of the drawing. Where do you notice contrast? Tension? Repetition? Disturbance? Incongruence?

PONDER. Consider how the problem of a patch is still a powerful metaphor for today.

PRAY. Turn your eyes upon Jesus in prayer. How is he offering something brand-new that is much stronger and more permanent than a patch for your life?

REFLECT. Rather than patching up your old way of life, what would it mean for you to put on a new way of life, like fine silk fit for the wedding feast of the King?

LIVE. How is Jesus inviting you to live life in such a way that it becomes congruent with his declaration that "this is Kingdom Come!" (Matthew 9:15)?

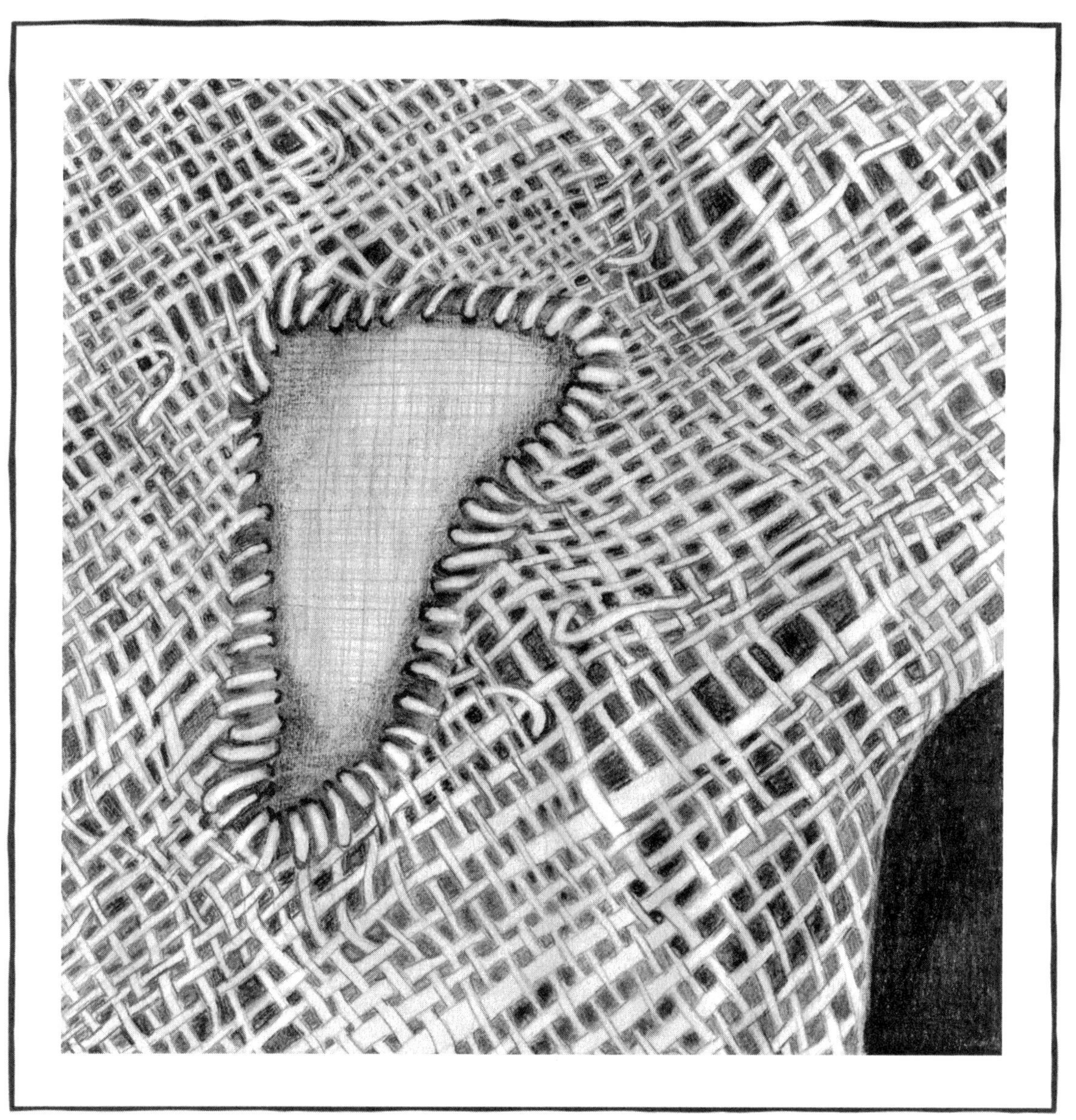

THE PATCH

4

NEW WINE IN CRACKED BOTTLES

Matthew 9:16-17; Mark 2:21-22; Luke 5:36-39

• • • • • • • • •

Jesus offers this parable at the same time he suggests that old cloth cannot be patched with new cloth or eventually it will tear. He's doubling up his efforts to speak parabolically and make one significant point with two parallel conclusions. The new—Jesus—has come to fulfill the ancient and prophetic messianic promises of old.

SIMILE. An intact bottle (or new wineskin) is the object of choice for Jesus to illustrate the significance of a fresh presentation of the Kingdom of God. New wine in cracked bottles doesn't cut it. Instead of placing new wine into an old bottle or skin, if you allow it to ferment, it will ultimately taste better coming from strong, new containers—one for aging and another for serving.

CONTRAST. It's all about the bottles. The old represents the religious practices, traditions, and structures of first-century Judaism. The new represents the new ways that are suitable to hold and pour out the teachings of Jesus. Are we to put new wine into cracked bottles? No! Are we to put new wine into new bottles? Yes!

LECTIO DIVINA

PAUSE. Sit silently and reverently with the Lord and invite him to make his presence known to you during this prayerfully reflective experience.

READ. Read the parable of Jesus a few times, either silently or aloud. Begin to notice what words and/or phrases pop off the page and land in your heart.

PONDER. Meditate on the parable, lingering with each word on the page. Note what's being formed in your heart and mind around the meaning of the parable.

PRAY. Formulate a prayer based on what you're noticing in the parable. Pay particular attention to the prompting of the Spirit toward one aspect of the parable.

REFLECT. Hold the parable like a diamond or a prism, looking at it from as many angles as possible. Notice any nuance or texture to the parable that feels invitational.

LIVE. Incarnate the truth you've discovered for your life today. Ask the Lord if there is one aspect of today's parable that you need to emulate in your sphere of influence. Or simply receive the parable as a gift for your soul.

NEW WINE IN CRACKED BOTTLES

Matthew 9:16-17

He went on, "No one cuts up a fine silk scarf to patch old work clothes; you want fabrics that match. And you don't put your wine in cracked bottles."

See also Mark 2:21-22; Luke 5:36-39

VISIO DIVINA

PAUSE. Ask the Lord to further unfold the passage with this image, *Wineskins*.

SEE. View what would have been an everyday household sight in ancient times. Compare and contrast what you notice in the two types of containers for wine—one for fermentation, the other for serving.

PONDER. Consider how it was common knowledge in Jesus' time that old wineskins (animal skins) already stretched out from the fermentation process were not suitable to be used again. What is like an old wineskin in your life that needs to be replaced with the new way of life that Jesus is inviting you into?

PRAY. Listen with the Lord, and talk to him about what you are wondering and what you are noticing.

REFLECT. Glance again at the drawing, considering, *What makes a good container for what God is forming in me, and what makes a good container for serving?*

LIVE. What is the Lord putting on your heart about being a suitable container for the new wine of the Kingdom?

WINESKINS

5

THE WEEDS

Matthew 13:24-30, 36-43

. . . .

Jesus addresses the crowd gathered by the Sea of Galilee from a small boat offshore. This is one of several parables found in Matthew 13 that reflect the Kingdom priorities of Jesus. At this time, his teaching ministry is experiencing a robust attraction from those who live nearby. When he later explains the parable to his disciples, he is in a home.

SIMILE. Jesus builds the story on the farmer who planted good seed into the good soil of his field. The farmer is obviously Jesus himself, and the field is ripe for the clean seed he plants. The field represents the world, in which the people of the Kingdom reside. Right next to the good seed are thistles planted by the enemy of their souls.

CONTRAST. Addressing good and evil in this world, Jesus acknowledges that weeds are allowed to coexist and seek to disrupt the growth of the Kingdom of Heaven here on earth. Eventually, however, the judgment will weed them out, and they will be collected, tied in bundles, and burned. This will be followed by the wheat being harvested by angels.

LECTIO DIVINA

PAUSE. Sit silently and reverently with the Lord and invite him to make his presence known to you during this prayerfully reflective experience.

READ. Read the parable of Jesus a few times, either silently or aloud. Begin to notice what words and/or phrases pop off the page and land in your heart.

PONDER. Meditate on the parable, lingering with each word on the page. Note what's being formed in your heart and mind around the meaning of the parable.

PRAY. Formulate a prayer based on what you're noticing in the parable. Pay particular attention to the prompting of the Spirit toward one aspect of the parable.

REFLECT. Hold the parable like a diamond or a prism, looking at it from as many angles as possible. Notice any nuance or texture to the parable that feels invitational.

LIVE. Incarnate the truth you've discovered for your life today. Ask the Lord if there is one aspect of today's parable that you need to emulate in your sphere of influence. Or simply receive the parable as a gift for your soul.

THE WEEDS

Matthew 13:24-30, 36-43

He told another story. "God's kingdom is like a farmer who planted good seed in his field. That night, while his hired men were asleep, his enemy sowed thistles all through the wheat and slipped away before dawn. When the first green shoots appeared and the grain began to form, the thistles showed up, too.

"The farmhands came to the farmer and said, 'Master, that was clean seed you planted, wasn't it? Where did these thistles come from?'

"He answered, 'Some enemy did this.'

"The farmhands asked, 'Should we weed out the thistles?'

"He said, 'No, if you weed the thistles, you'll pull up the wheat, too. Let them grow together until harvest time. Then I'll instruct the harvesters to pull up the thistles and tie them in bundles for the fire, then gather the wheat and put it in the barn.'" . . .

Jesus dismissed the congregation and went into the house. His disciples came in and said, "Explain to us that story of the thistles in the field."

So he explained. "The farmer who sows the pure seed is the Son of Man. The field is the world, the pure seeds are subjects of the kingdom, the thistles are subjects of the Devil, and the enemy who sows them is the Devil. The harvest is the end of the age, the curtain of history. The harvest hands are angels.

"The picture of thistles pulled up and burned is a scene from the final act. The Son of Man will send his angels, weed out the thistles from his kingdom, pitch them in the trash, and be done with them. They are going to complain to high heaven, but nobody is going to listen. At the same time, ripe, holy lives will mature and adorn the kingdom of their Father.

"Are you listening to this? Really listening?"

VISIO DIVINA

PAUSE. Simply rest a moment with the Lord, remembering what stood out to you in this parable. Stay with it as you pray with this drawing, *Imposters among the Wheat.*

SEE. Take time to carefully observe the drawing. Can you find the imposters among the wheat? What differences and similarities do you observe? What does the wheat's proximity to the imposters make you wonder?

PONDER. Is there anything that surprises you about the parable? How might this parable provide wisdom for living in proximity to those who do not share your faith?

PRAY. Talk to the Lord about what is stirring in you as you consider this parable.

REFLECT. What is it like to consider yourself as wheat growing up in proximity to thistles, weeds, or wheat imposters? What is the temptation? What is the invitation?

LIVE. What change in perspective might the Lord be working in your heart? How would you like it to affect the way you live?

IMPOSTERS AMONG THE WHEAT

6

THE MUSTARD SEED/ACORN

Matthew 13:31-32; Mark 4:30-32; Luke 13:18-19

. . . .

Jesus continues to speak in parables to the crowd that has assembled. He knows that these people have at least a fleeting interest in the Kingdom of God. With their well-being in mind, he speaks from his heart, reminding them of eternal truths made available for them to claim—one seed at a time.

SIMILE. While this story is commonly known as the parable of the mustard seed, in *The Message* Eugene Peterson prefers the metaphor of the acorn. Both seeds are miniscule compared to what they grow into. The mustard seed germinates quickly into the mustard tree, becoming the largest in the garden. The acorn matures into an oak tree, the strongest tree in the forest.

CONTRAST. The picture of contrast that Jesus is painting has to do with size. What may seem small to the naked eye can actually grow to become something grand. Jesus is noting here that something hidden and mysterious is happening underground as the seeds of his Kingdom are being planted. Seeds of hope grow and multiply plentifully.

LECTIO DIVINA

· · · · · · · · ·

PAUSE. Sit silently and reverently with the Lord and invite him to make his presence known to you during this prayerfully reflective experience.

READ. Read the parable of Jesus a few times, either silently or aloud. Begin to notice what words and/or phrases pop off the page and land in your heart.

PONDER. Meditate on the parable, lingering with each word on the page. Note what's being formed in your heart and mind around the meaning of the parable.

PRAY. Formulate a prayer based on what you're noticing in the parable. Pay particular attention to the prompting of the Spirit toward one aspect of the parable.

REFLECT. Hold the parable like a diamond or a prism, looking at it from as many angles as possible. Notice any nuance or texture to the parable that feels invitational.

LIVE. Incarnate the truth you've discovered for your life today. Ask the Lord if there is one aspect of today's parable that you need to emulate in your sphere of influence. Or simply receive the parable as a gift for your soul.

THE MUSTARD SEED/ACORN

Matthew 13:31-32

Another story. "God's kingdom is like an acorn that a farmer plants. It is quite small as seeds go, but in the course of years it grows into a huge oak tree, and eagles build nests in it."

See also Mark 4:30-32; Luke 13:18-19

VISIO DIVINA

· · · · · · · · ·

PAUSE. Ask the Lord to open the eyes of your heart as you sit with this drawing, *The Mustard Seed and the Acorn.*

SEE. What catches your eye when you first look at this drawing? Let your eyes pause and focus on what you see. How does the design give emphasis to the themes of size and proportion?

PONDER. What goes on inside you as you ponder humble beginnings, slow growth through the passage of time, and the promise of great fruitfulness? How might this connect with your own story in some way?

PRAY. Simply quiet yourself before the Lord as you wonder with him about small seeds he may be planting in your soul.

REFLECT. What emerged in the quiet of your prayer? Gaze upon the drawing once more, reflecting on the transformation, the strength, the size, and the hospitality of the tree. What insight or longing stirs in you about the Kingdom of God?

LIVE. How is this parable a gift for your life today?

THE MUSTARD SEED AND THE ACORN

53

7

THE YEAST

Matthew 13:33; Luke 13:20-21

· · · · · · · · ·

Found within the series of parables recorded for us in Matthew 13 (and again in Luke 13) is the parable of the yeast (or leaven). Jesus is speaking with passion and clarity about the pervasive, transformative nature of the Kingdom of God. Jesus is serious about its significance, and he earnestly desires for all to believe the Good News.

SIMILE. The use of yeast as Jesus' chosen metaphor highlights the hidden yet powerful role leaven plays in the bread kneaded by the woman. The yeast represents the Kingdom of Heaven. The woman is the one working the yeast into the flour, signifying those with quiet, invisible, and profound Kingdom influence in our world.

CONTRAST. The woman in this parable needs great strength to be able to mix the yeast into about sixty pounds of flour. The toil necessary to spread the yeast appropriately speaks to both the human effort of kneading and the hidden work of permeation of the yeast into the dough. Something as small as yeast has a great impact when it's well distributed and given time to rise.

LECTIO DIVINA

PAUSE. Sit silently and reverently with the Lord and invite him to make his presence known to you during this prayerfully reflective experience.

READ. Read the parable of Jesus a few times, either silently or aloud. Begin to notice what words and/or phrases pop off the page and land in your heart.

PONDER. Meditate on the parable, lingering with each word on the page. Note what's being formed in your heart and mind around the meaning of the parable.

PRAY. Formulate a prayer based on what you're noticing in the parable. Pay particular attention to the prompting of the Spirit toward one aspect of the parable.

REFLECT. Hold the parable like a diamond or a prism, looking at it from as many angles as possible. Notice any nuance or texture to the parable that feels invitational.

LIVE. Incarnate the truth you've discovered for your life today. Ask the Lord if there is one aspect of today's parable that you need to emulate in your sphere of influence. Or simply receive the parable as a gift for your soul.

THE YEAST

Matthew 13:33

Another story. "God's kingdom is like yeast that a woman works into the dough for dozens of loaves of barley bread—and waits while the dough rises."

See also Luke 13:20-21

VISIO DIVINA

PAUSE. As you make time to be attentive, welcome the Lord to be with you while looking at this drawing, *The Yeast*.

SEE. As you scan this scene, how do you see evidence of the yeast doing its work—in the foreground, the middle ground, and the background (depicted in a time-lapse window)? How does the artwork suggest a recipe for transformation?

PONDER. Consider the hiddenness of the active ingredient and its power to affect all the dough. How does this shape your view of God's Kingdom?

PRAY. Have a conversation with the Lord as you bring what you are noticing to him. (Consider following a yeast bread recipe as an all-day act of listening prayer.)

REFLECT. What is evoked in you as you reflect on the mysterious, active, and transformational work of God in your life?

What words or images come to mind as you contemplate what it means to cooperate with God in what he is doing?

LIVE. What is the Lord inviting you to be or to do in response?

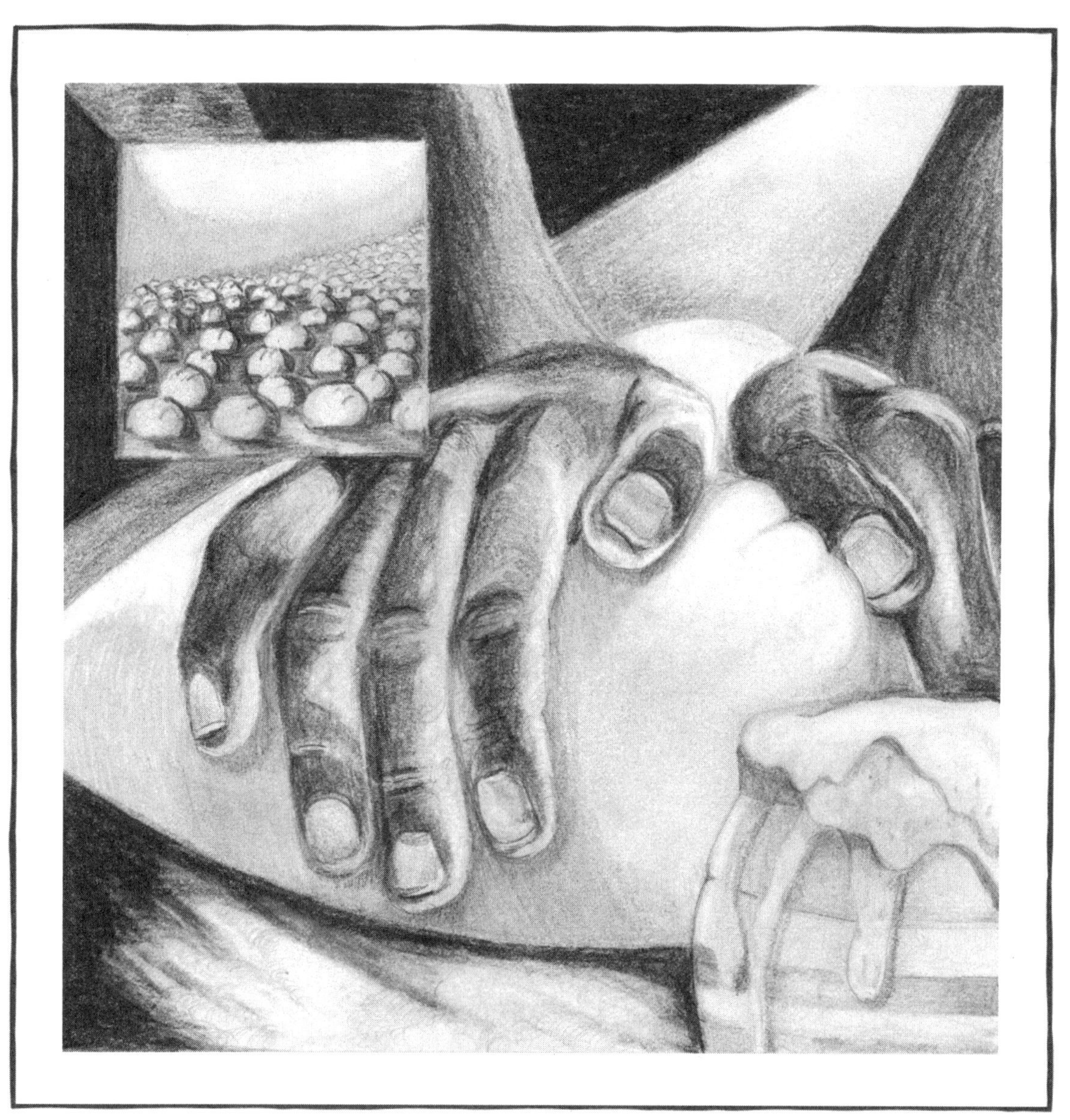

THE YEAST

8

THE HIDDEN TREASURE

Matthew 13:44

. . . .

As Jesus seeks to cement within the hearts of his hearers the truth of the Kingdom, he is consistently placing God's Kingdom over the world's kingdom. Repeatedly, in specific and unique stories, Jesus underscores the central reason why he has come to live among them: to proclaim the Kingdom of God. Seek this treasure—hidden but in plain sight.

SIMILE. A hidden treasure in a field. Left there long ago. Accidentally found by a trespasser, who immediately sees the value of the treasure and ecstatically celebrates his discovery. So he digs a hole and places the treasure therein. With joy, he goes and sells all he has in order to buy the field and ultimately the treasure buried in it.

CONTRAST. Hidden and found. Buried and revealed. Accidentally and purposefully. Sell everything in order to purchase and own the field. Rich with a treasure trove of meaning, this parable speaks of the joy of discovery and the delight of sacrificial expense. Once we have discovered the Kingdom of God, there's no turning back.

LECTIO DIVINA

PAUSE. Sit silently and reverently with the Lord and invite him to make his presence known to you during this prayerfully reflective experience.

READ. Read the parable of Jesus a few times, either silently or aloud. Begin to notice what words and/or phrases pop off the page and land in your heart.

PONDER. Meditate on the parable, lingering with each word on the page. Note what's being formed in your heart and mind around the meaning of the parable.

PRAY. Formulate a prayer based on what you're noticing in the parable. Pay particular attention to the prompting of the Spirit toward one aspect of the parable.

REFLECT. Hold the parable like a diamond or a prism, looking at it from as many angles as possible. Notice any nuance or texture to the parable that feels invitational.

LIVE. Incarnate the truth you've discovered for your life today. Ask the Lord if there is one aspect of today's parable that you need to emulate in your sphere of influence. Or simply receive the parable as a gift for your soul.

THE HIDDEN TREASURE

Matthew 13:44

"God's kingdom is like a treasure hidden in a field for years and then accidentally found by a trespasser. The finder is ecstatic—what a find!—and proceeds to sell everything he owns to raise money and buy that field."

<h1 style="text-align:center">VISIO DIVINA</h1>

• • • • • • • •

PAUSE. In a prayerful posture, open your heart to the Lord as you consider this drawing, *What a Find!*

SEE. Where does your eye settle first as you look at this drawing? Remain there for a while and notice what it causes you to wonder.

Scan the entire drawing, recalling the story told in the parable.

How do the angles and perspective of the treasure chest invite your involvement?

PONDER. Place yourself in the story. What God-given treasure would be so great that you would be willing to trade in all other treasures to have it?

PRAY. In the quiet of your prayer, be with the Lord in what you are holding in your heart and mind.

REFLECT. What is the Lord helping you see about your this-world treasures and how they compare with what God offers you?

LIVE. What would it be like to respond to Jesus by releasing a treasure that draws you away from God in exchange for a treasure that draws you toward him?

WHAT A FIND!

9

THE PEARL

Matthew 13:45-46

. . . .

By now, we feel the drumbeat of the parables Jesus expresses and Matthew records. Among a steady stream of Kingdom parables, the pearl (of great price) is yet another offering of Jesus to his followers. The pearl the merchant finds is flawless, just like Jesus himself—perfect, exquisite, and unblemished.

SIMILE. A jewel merchant is on the lookout for exquisite pearls. We can picture him holding a jeweler's loupe up to his right eye, magnifying and inspecting all possible candidates for the flawless one. Upon finding the one he's been searching for, he sells everything in order to buy it. Simply to have it in his hand to hold, admire, and appreciate. Not for resale.

CONTRAST. Fine jewels versus the flawless pearl. The jewel merchant knows the difference. Jewelry can be deceptive; is it the real thing or an imposter, a fake, or made with imitation jewel? Artificial materials are less expensive and designed to look costly, but to the trained eye, there is a big difference. Jesus is the flawless One, the Pearl of all pearls. Praise God!

LECTIO DIVINA

PAUSE. Sit silently and reverently with the Lord and invite him to make his presence known to you during this prayerfully reflective experience.

READ. Read the parable of Jesus a few times, either silently or aloud. Begin to notice what words and/or phrases pop off the page and land in your heart.

PONDER. Meditate on the parable, lingering with each word on the page. Note what's being formed in your heart and mind around the meaning of the parable.

PRAY. Formulate a prayer based on what you're noticing in the parable. Pay particular attention to the prompting of the Spirit toward one aspect of the parable.

REFLECT. Hold the parable like a diamond or a prism, looking at it from as many angles as possible. Notice any nuance or texture to the parable that feels invitational.

LIVE. Incarnate the truth you've discovered for your life today. Ask the Lord if there is one aspect of today's parable that you need to emulate in your sphere of influence. Or simply receive the parable as a gift for your soul.

THE PEARL

Matthew 13:45-46

"Or, God's kingdom is like a jewel merchant on the hunt for exquisite pearls. Finding one that is flawless, he immediately sells everything and buys it."

VISIO DIVINA

PAUSE. Remember the Lord's presence with you as you contemplate this rendering, *The Pearl.*

SEE. Gaze upon the miraculous beauty of an oyster shell and the treasure that is created inside. What do you see?

PONDER. Consider what it would be like to spend all of one's time, energy, resources, and passions in the search for something so beautiful and valuable—and then to find it!

PRAY. Close your eyes for a moment and turn your gaze upon the beauty of the Lord in your mind's eye. Prayerfully pause there, with God.

REFLECT. What emerged in the quiet of your prayer? Gaze upon the illustration once more, allowing it to become a glimpse of the beauty of the Lord in his creation.

LIVE. What God-given desire is beckoning you toward a seeking-and-finding way of life in the Kingdom of God?

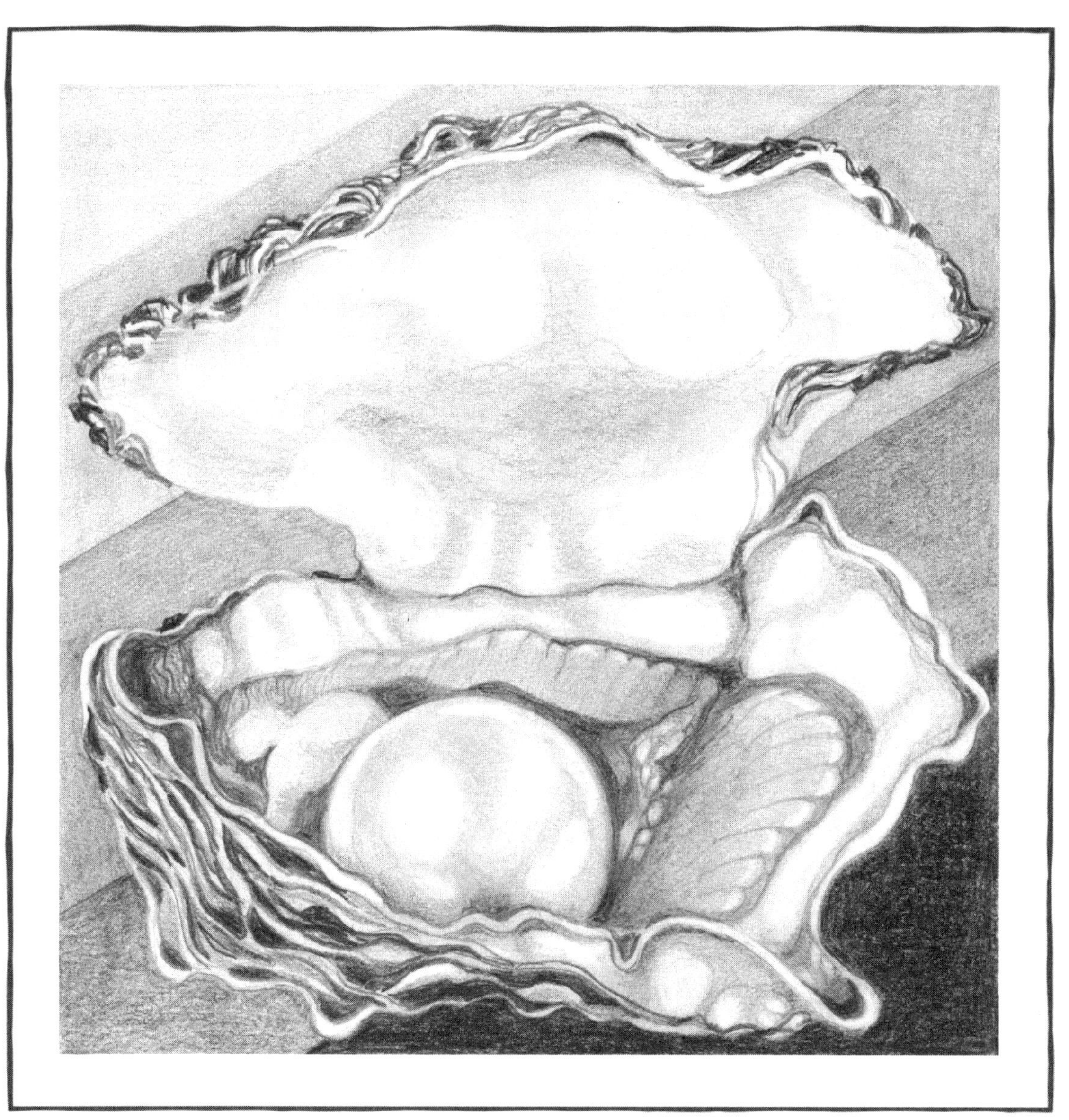

THE PEARL

10

THE NET

Matthew 13:47-50

· · · · · · · · ·

This message is hard to hear for the unrighteous. Whole generations of people groups have missed the point about calling on the name of the Lord. Unfortunately, they will face the wrath of God; when "the curtain comes down on history" (Matthew 13:49), the angels will cull the bad fish, and despite their complaining, will throw them onto a heap of garbage.

SIMILE. Jesus tells the story of a fishnet cast into the sea. It catches all kinds of fish. When it's full, it gets hauled onto the beach, where the good ones are plucked and placed in a bucket. The unfit-to-eat fish are thrown away. So it will be when the end of the age comes and the angels do their work of separation, the wicked from the righteous.

CONTRAST. Good fish. Bad fish. Saved or thrown away. Righteous or unrighteous. Ending up on the right side of history or complaining about the judgment with weeping and gnashing of teeth. Jesus couldn't have been clearer about the end. And he illuminates its importance in simple stories. The end will come. For good. For evil. Forever.

LECTIO DIVINA

· · · · · · · · ·

PAUSE. Sit silently and reverently with the Lord and invite him to make his presence known to you during this prayerfully reflective experience.

READ. Read the parable of Jesus a few times, either silently or aloud. Begin to notice what words and/or phrases pop off the page and land in your heart.

PONDER. Meditate on the parable, lingering with each word on the page. Note what's being formed in your heart and mind around the meaning of the parable.

PRAY. Formulate a prayer based on what you're noticing in the parable. Pay particular attention to the prompting of the Spirit toward one aspect of the parable.

REFLECT. Hold the parable like a diamond or a prism, looking at it from as many angles as possible. Notice any nuance or texture to the parable that feels invitational.

LIVE. Incarnate the truth you've discovered for your life today. Ask the Lord if there is one aspect of today's parable that you need to emulate in your sphere of influence. Or simply receive the parable as a gift for your soul.

THE NET

Matthew 13:47-50

"Or, God's kingdom is like a fishnet cast into the sea, catching all kinds of fish. When it is full, it is hauled onto the beach. The good fish are picked out and put in a tub; those unfit to eat are thrown away. That's how it will be when the curtain comes down on history. The angels will come and cull the bad fish and throw them in the garbage. There will be a lot of desperate complaining, but it won't do any good."

VISIO DIVINA

PAUSE. Ask the Lord to guide you as you pray with this image, *The Net*.

SEE. What is your eye drawn to as you look at the artwork?

How does the artwork portray the impending reckoning, "when the curtain comes down on history" (Matthew 13:49)?

PONDER. What is it like for you to consider God's Kingdom as being like a full fishnet?

PRAY. Look away from the drawing. In your mind's eye, see yourself with Jesus at the end of the age. What do you want to say to him or ask of him?

REFLECT. Look upon the image of the fishnet again. When you consider the character of the One who is telling the parable and his merciful mission, what is the range of emotion that accompanies your thoughts?

LIVE. How might the Lord be inviting you into a new perspective or a changed focus about Kingdom life with God?

THE NET

THE STORE OWNER

Matthew 13:52

• • • • • • • •

This parable concludes the rivulet of parables offered in Matthew 13. This time, the focus is on the disciples who become teachers of God's Word. Jesus is reinforcing the value of both the ancient and the modern riches of their teaching. The old treasures of Jewish law and the new treasures of Jesus provide a holistic grasp of the Scriptures.

SIMILE. The parable features a store owner (or a homeowner in other translations) who effortlessly brings out of his storeroom both old and new treasures. A judicious teacher of God's Word, or a committed disciple of Jesus, is to do likewise. With wisdom and discernment, the treasures of the Law and the Prophets are to be combined with the new treasures found in Jesus.

CONTRAST. Old treasures and new. No longer hidden but brought out of the storeroom to be shared with all. No longer hoarding one or the other but serving as a faithful witness to both the old and the new. A redeemed owner—a teacher of the biblical story of faith—compelled to generously share the richness of God's treasures.

LECTIO DIVINA

• • • • • • • • •

PAUSE. Sit silently and reverently with the Lord and invite him to make his presence known to you during this prayerfully reflective experience.

READ. Read the parable of Jesus a few times, either silently or aloud. Begin to notice what words and/or phrases pop off the page and land in your heart.

PONDER. Meditate on the parable, lingering with each word on the page. Note what's being formed in your heart and mind around the meaning of the parable.

PRAY. Formulate a prayer based on what you're noticing in the parable. Pay particular attention to the prompting of the Spirit toward one aspect of the parable.

REFLECT. Hold the parable like a diamond or a prism, looking at it from as many angles as possible. Notice any nuance or texture to the parable that feels invitational.

LIVE. Incarnate the truth you've discovered for your life today. Ask the Lord if there is one aspect of today's parable that you need to emulate in your sphere of influence. Or simply receive the parable as a gift for your soul.

THE STORE OWNER

Matthew 13:52

He said, "Then you see how every student well-trained in God's kingdom is like the owner of a general store who can put his hands on anything you need, old or new, exactly when you need it."

VISIO DIVINA

PAUSE. Ask the Lord for insight into his Word as you spend time with this piece of artwork, *Rolled Away and Lifted Up*.

SEE. Gaze upon the parallel windows of the storeroom, depicting treasures of the old fulfilled by the new treasures of Jesus. What do you notice? How do the symbols of old and new, side by side, invite you into awe and wonder and gratitude for the big picture of God's rescue and gift of new life?

PONDER. Ponder the treasure of both old and new. For example: "In the same way that Moses lifted the serpent in the desert so people could have something to see and then believe, it is necessary for the Son of Man to be lifted up—and everyone who looks up to him, trusting and expectant, will gain a real life, eternal life" (John 3:14-15). And in the same way that the waters of the Red Sea were rolled away to deliver the people out of slavery, the stone at the tomb of Jesus was rolled away for our deliverance.

PRAY. Bring what you are noticing into a prayerful place of praise and thankfulness. What do you want to say to Jesus?

REFLECT. How is your life with Jesus helping you become a "student well-trained in God's kingdom" (Matthew 13:52)? How is Jesus inviting you into more of an experiential knowledge of his storeroom of treasures in the Scriptures?

LIVE. What spiritual practice would you like to engage in as you respond to the promptings of this parable?

ROLLED AWAY AND LIFTED UP

I 2

THE UNMERCIFUL SERVANT

Matthew 18:23-35

. . . .

The central theme in this string of teachings is forgiveness. Jesus is addressing his disciples, answering Peter's specific question "Master, how many times do I forgive a brother or sister who hurts me? Seven?" (Matthew 18:21). Not surprisingly, Jesus' answer is extravagant: not seven times but seventy times seven times.

SIMILE. Forgiveness is to be offered to another in the unconditional manner of God's mercy and grace. Do unto others as you've been done unto. Forgive your debtors as you've been forgiven of your own debts. Forgive not once but seventy times seven times. There is no acceptable alternative to forgiveness. Jesus knows it's difficult but essential to offer. Always.

CONTRAST. The king in this story sets a powerful example for his servants in his dramatic expression of absolute, unconditional forgiveness. Not only is the king's forgiveness and his servant's unforgiveness a picture of contrast, but so is the amount of debt owed and the extent of forgiveness required. The forgiven servant, unwilling to show mercy to his fellow servant, completely misses the point.

LECTIO DIVINA

PAUSE. Sit silently and reverently with the Lord and invite him to make his presence known to you during this prayerfully reflective experience.

READ. Read the parable of Jesus a few times, either silently or aloud. Begin to notice what words and/or phrases pop off the page and land in your heart.

PONDER. Meditate on the parable, lingering with each word on the page. Note what's being formed in your heart and mind around the meaning of the parable.

PRAY. Formulate a prayer based on what you're noticing in the parable. Pay particular attention to the prompting of the Spirit toward one aspect of the parable.

REFLECT. Hold the parable like a diamond or a prism, looking at it from as many angles as possible. Notice any nuance or texture to the parable that feels invitational.

LIVE. Incarnate the truth you've discovered for your life today. Ask the Lord if there is one aspect of today's parable that you need to emulate in your sphere of influence. Or simply receive the parable as a gift for your soul.

THE UNMERCIFUL SERVANT

Matthew 18:23-35

"The kingdom of God is like a king who decided to square accounts with his servants. As he got under way, one servant was brought before him who had run up a debt of a hundred thousand dollars. He couldn't pay up, so the king ordered the man, along with his wife, children, and goods, to be auctioned off at the slave market.

"The poor wretch threw himself at the king's feet and begged, 'Give me a chance and I'll pay it all back.' Touched by his plea, the king let him off, erasing the debt.

"The servant was no sooner out of the room when he came upon one of his fellow servants who owed him ten dollars. He seized him by the throat and demanded, 'Pay up. Now!'

"The poor wretch threw himself down and begged, 'Give me a chance and I'll pay it all back.' But he wouldn't do it. He had him arrested and put in jail until the debt was paid. When the other servants saw this going on, they were outraged and brought a detailed report to the king.

"The king summoned the man and said, 'You evil servant! I forgave your entire debt when you begged me for mercy. Shouldn't you be compelled to be merciful to your fellow servant who asked for mercy?' The king was furious and put the screws to the man until he paid back his entire debt. And that's exactly what my Father in heaven is going to do to each one of you who doesn't forgive unconditionally anyone who asks for mercy."

VISIO DIVINA

PAUSE. Ask God's Spirit to move inside your heart and mind as you consider this drawing, *Forgiveness*.

SEE. Look over the drawing, searching for symbols. How does the simple symbolism of human gesture, light and darkness, numbers, words, and even fonts evoke a personal connection with the parable? How do these symbols of forgiveness transcend time and invite your involvement in the story?

PONDER. More than a piece of paper, the profound need to receive and offer forgiveness has run deep in the human condition since the beginning of time. In your life, how have you been forgiven? Where do you desire forgiveness? Whom do you need help from God to forgive? What relationships come to mind for you?

PRAY. How many times do we pray, *Forgive us our sins as we forgive those who sin against us* (see Matthew 6:12) so quickly that our hearts don't even have a chance to catch up with our words? Take some time to stay in this prayer that Jesus taught us to pray while listening—*really* listening—to your heart and to Jesus' heart for you.

REFLECT. Where do you need courage and strength from God to live a life of being forgiven and being one who forgives?

LIVE. How do you want to trust God today in taking the next step toward forgiveness in your relationships?

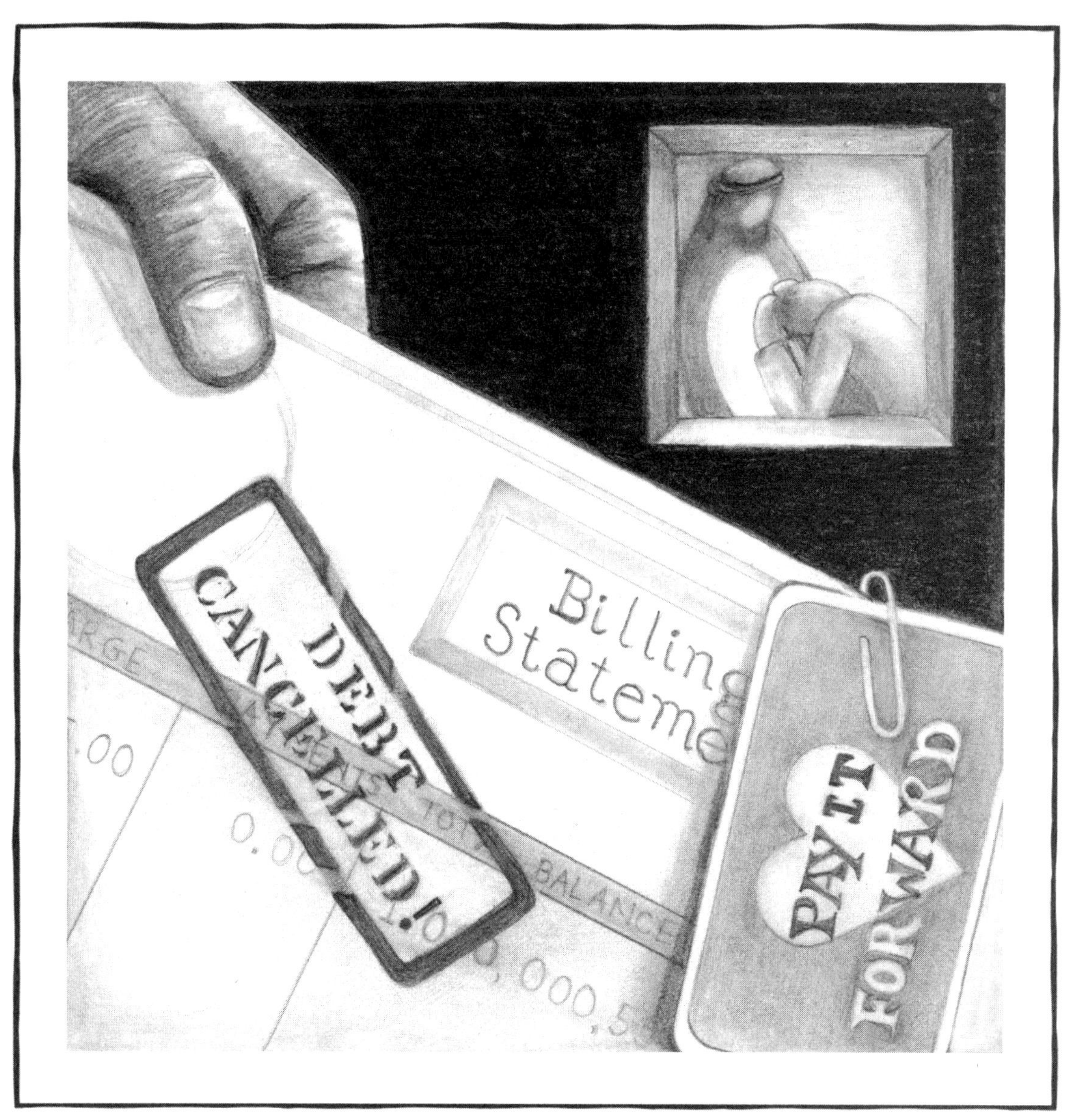

FORGIVENESS

13

THE WORKERS IN THE VINEYARD

Matthew 20:1-16

. . . .

This story follows Jesus' teachings about the dangers of wealth and the cost of discipleship. Wanting to know the reward for leaving everything to follow Jesus, Peter asks, "What do we get out of it?" (Matthew 19:27). Jesus replies that there will be a "Great Reversal": The first will be last, and the last will be first (Matthew 19:30). The vineyard workers, no matter when they show up, receive the same wage.

SIMILE. The Kingdom of Heaven is like an estate manager who hires workers for his vineyard. Every worker, regardless of when during the day they are employed, agrees to their wage: one dollar. Everyone gets the same pay regardless of the amount of time they work in the vineyard. So it is in God's Kingdom-reward budget. But all who hear are flummoxed.

CONTRAST. The workers in the vineyard grumble and grouse about the generosity of the landowner. They are filled with anger because of the system of reward determined and activated by the manager. Confronting their heart attitude of envy and frustration, they are reminded of the leader's fairness. Each party initially affirmed and has now fulfilled their agreed-upon terms of employment.

LECTIO DIVINA

· · · · · · · · ·

PAUSE. Sit silently and reverently with the Lord and invite him to make his presence known to you during this prayerfully reflective experience.

READ. Read the parable of Jesus a few times, either silently or aloud. Begin to notice what words and/or phrases pop off the page and land in your heart.

PONDER. Meditate on the parable, lingering with each word on the page. Note what's being formed in your heart and mind around the meaning of the parable.

PRAY. Formulate a prayer based on what you're noticing in the parable. Pay particular attention to the prompting of the Spirit toward one aspect of the parable.

REFLECT. Hold the parable like a diamond or a prism, looking at it from as many angles as possible. Notice any nuance or texture to the parable that feels invitational.

LIVE. Incarnate the truth you've discovered for your life today. Ask the Lord if there is one aspect of today's parable that you need to emulate in your sphere of influence. Or simply receive the parable as a gift for your soul.

THE WORKERS IN THE VINEYARD

Matthew 20:1-16

"God's kingdom is like an estate manager who went out early in the morning to hire workers for his vineyard. They agreed on a wage of a dollar a day, and went to work.

"Later, about nine o'clock, the manager saw some other men hanging around the town square unemployed. He told them to go to work in his vineyard and he would pay them a fair wage. They went.

"He did the same thing at noon, and again at three o'clock. At five o'clock he went back and found still others standing around. He said, 'Why are you standing around all day doing nothing?'

"They said, 'Because no one hired us.'

"He told them to go to work in his vineyard.

"When the day's work was over, the owner of the vineyard instructed his foreman, 'Call the workers in and pay them their wages. Start with the last hired and go on to the first.'

"Those hired at five o'clock came up and were each given a dollar. When those who were hired first saw that, they assumed they would get far more. But they got the same, each of them one dollar. Taking the dollar, they groused angrily to the manager, 'These last workers put in only one easy hour, and you just made them equal to us, who slaved all day under a scorching sun.'

"He replied to the one speaking for the rest, 'Friend, I haven't been unfair. We agreed on the wage of a dollar, didn't we? So take it and go. I decided to give to the one who came last the same as you. Can't I do what I want with my own money? Are you going to get stingy because I am generous?'

"Here it is again, the Great Reversal: many of the first ending up last, and the last first."

VISIO DIVINA

PAUSE. Remain in a prayerful posture as you focus on this drawing, *Wages or Gift?*

SEE. Observe how the movement of the design takes you from sunrise to sunset, undergirded and anchored in the nearness of God's faithful hand of provision. Allow the picture to help you stay with the parable in new ways.

PONDER. As the artwork's title suggests, many questions arise, depending on the perspective and the values one holds. As you ponder this story, what questions arise in you? What values and perspectives provoke those questions?

PRAY. Jesus understands what drives our questions. Come to him with your honest queries.

REFLECT. What is it about the upside-down, first-shall-be-last Kingdom of God that is most refreshing to you? Conversely, what is most challenging for you?

LIVE. Where do you notice your God-given desires for grateful and gracious living, and how do you want to look to Jesus for his guidance?

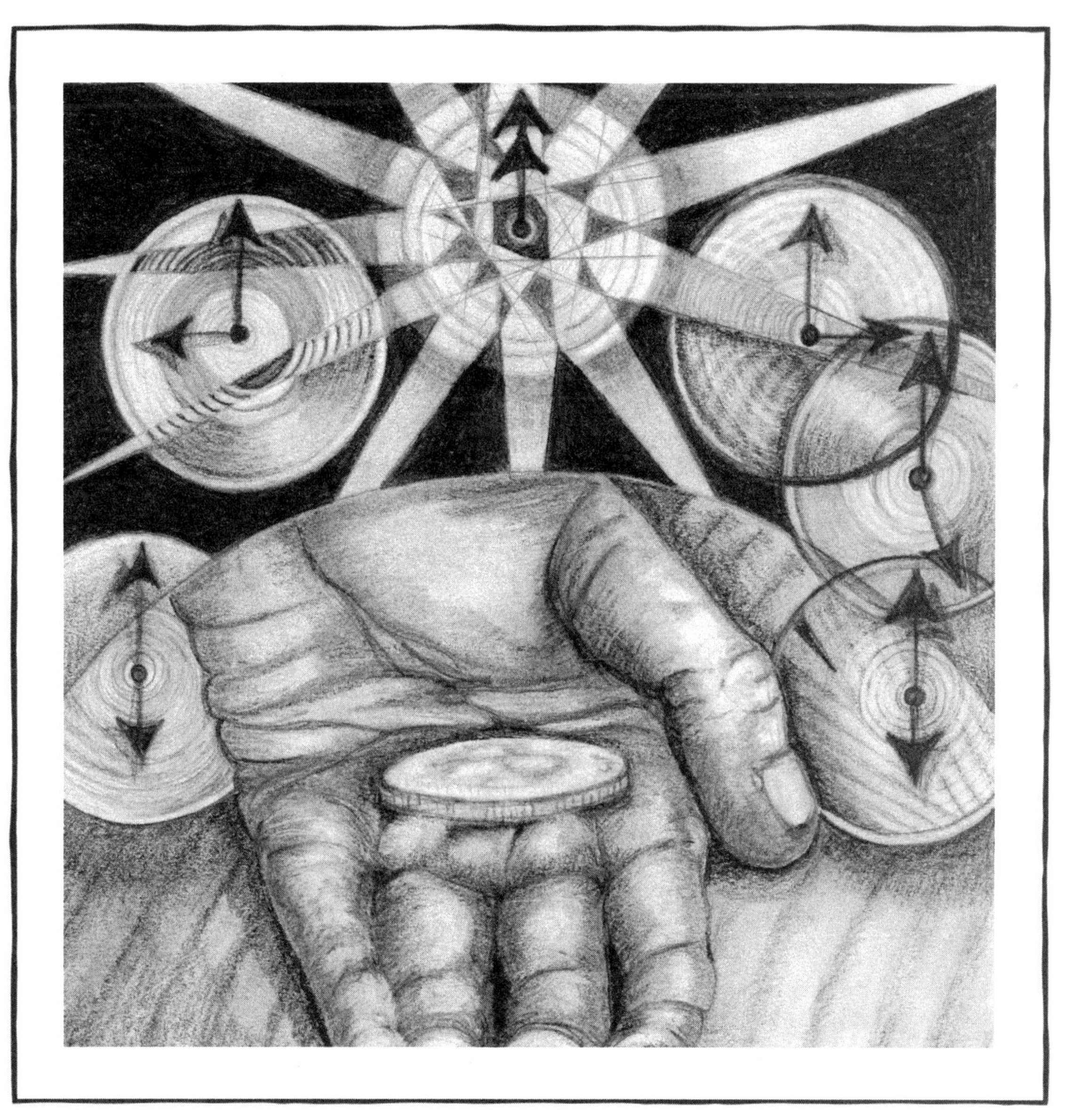

WAGES OR GIFT?

14

THE TWO SONS

Matthew 21:28-32

• • • • • • • • •

In a series of teachings on the Kingdom, within the Temple courts, Jesus is speaking to the religious leaders of the day who are confronting his authority. His heart and mind are fixed on the Kingdom he has come to proclaim. Sinners come to recognize their need for God while the leaders of the day scoff defiantly.

SIMILE. One son initially denies his father's wish for him to go and work in the vineyard but later changes his mind and does so. The other son initially responds positively to the father's request but doesn't follow through. Jesus asks the religious leaders, "Which of the two sons did what the father asked?" (Matthew 21:31). They answer correctly—"The first"—but miss the point completely.

CONTRAST. The two sons expose two distinct heart motivations. Repentance is true remorse and complete turning away from sin. Hypocrisy upends genuine obedience with shallow cynicism and lip service to the discipline required to fol-low Jesus. The pride of the religious rulers of Jesus' day stands in stark polarity to the genuine humility Jesus models and invites among his followers.

LECTIO DIVINA

PAUSE. Sit silently and reverently with the Lord and invite him to make his presence known to you during this prayerfully reflective experience.

READ. Read the parable of Jesus a few times, either silently or aloud. Begin to notice what words and/or phrases pop off the page and land in your heart.

PONDER. Meditate on the parable, lingering with each word on the page. Note what's being formed in your heart and mind around the meaning of the parable.

PRAY. Formulate a prayer based on what you're noticing in the parable. Pay particular attention to the prompting of the Spirit toward one aspect of the parable.

REFLECT. Hold the parable like a diamond or a prism, looking at it from as many angles as possible. Notice any nuance or texture to the parable that feels invitational.

LIVE. Incarnate the truth you've discovered for your life today. Ask the Lord if there is one aspect of today's parable that you need to emulate in your sphere of influence. Or simply receive the parable as a gift for your soul.

THE TWO SONS
Matthew 21:28-32

"Tell me what you think of this story: A man had two sons. He went up to the first and said, 'Son, go out for the day and work in the vineyard.'

"The son answered, 'I don't want to.' Later on he thought better of it and went.

"The father gave the same command to the second son. He answered, 'Sure, glad to.' But he never went.

"Which of the two sons did what the father asked?"

They said, "The first."

Jesus said, "Yes, and I tell you that crooks and whores are going to precede you into God's kingdom. John came to you showing you the right road. You turned up your noses at him, but the crooks and whores believed him. Even when you saw their changed lives, you didn't care enough to change and believe him."

VISIO DIVINA

PAUSE. Stop for a moment to recenter your thoughts on Jesus as you pray with this piece of artwork, *The Two Sons*.

SEE. How does your eye move through the design? How do the lines, angles, and contrast emphasize the movement of the story? When the pace of your observation begins to slow down, where does your eye want to rest in the design?

PONDER. What stirs in you as you ponder this parable? Which son do you sense a connection to in your life with God right now?

PRAY. What would you like to talk about with Jesus? Have a conversation with him about what's on your mind and in your heart.

REFLECT. If God's Spirit is moving in you or prompting you, how do you want to respond? What spiritual practices help you open up to God's help for moving from good intentions to follow-through?

LIVE. What would it look like today to decide to reverse your posture and turn around toward something God is inviting you to?

THE TWO SONS

15

THE TENANTS

Matthew 21:33-45; Mark 12:1-12; Luke 20:9-19

. . . .

In this parable, we find Jesus in the Temple courts in Jerusalem. He is addressing the chief priests, Pharisees, and all who have serious questions about his apparent authority. He knows that his earthly ministry will soon be complete. Justice and judgment await all who turn against the Kingdom of God and its chief cornerstone, Jesus.

SIMILE. A wealthy farmer or vineyard owner is the central figure in this story. It's obvious that Jesus is referencing God as the owner, as is the case in other parables. The owner has many servants who attempt to collect from the tenants at harvest time, but each is met with their own calamity. The tenants reject God's messengers, even his beloved son.

CONTRAST. The wealthy farmer and the wicked tenants stand on opposite sides of the work, will, and way of Jesus. Unfaithful, arrogant, and damning disobedience is on display here in a story with a dramatic conclusion: Reject God and his messengers, and the consequences will be eternal. God's sovereignty and justice will always reign supreme.

LECTIO DIVINA

PAUSE. Sit silently and reverently with the Lord and invite him to make his presence known to you during this prayerfully reflective experience.

READ. Read the parable of Jesus a few times, either silently or aloud. Begin to notice what words and/or phrases pop off the page and land in your heart.

PONDER. Meditate on the parable, lingering with each word on the page. Note what's being formed in your heart and mind around the meaning of the parable.

PRAY. Formulate a prayer based on what you're noticing in the parable. Pay particular attention to the prompting of the Spirit toward one aspect of the parable.

REFLECT. Hold the parable like a diamond or a prism, looking at it from as many angles as possible. Notice any nuance or texture to the parable that feels invitational.

LIVE. Incarnate the truth you've discovered for your life today. Ask the Lord if there is one aspect of today's parable that you need to emulate in your sphere of influence. Or simply receive the parable as a gift for your soul.

THE TENANTS

Matthew 21:33-45

"Here's another story. Listen closely. There was once a man, a wealthy farmer, who planted a vineyard. He fenced it, dug a winepress, put up a watchtower, then turned it over to the farmhands and went off on a trip. When it was time to harvest the grapes, he sent his servants back to collect his profits.

"The farmhands grabbed the first servant and beat him up. The next one they murdered. They threw stones at the third but he got away. The owner tried again, sending more servants. They got the same treatment. The owner was at the end of his rope. He decided to send his son. 'Surely,' he thought, 'they will respect my son.'

"But when the farmhands saw the son arrive, they rubbed their hands in greed. 'This is the heir! Let's kill him and have it all for ourselves.' They grabbed him, threw him out, and killed him.

"Now, when the owner of the vineyard arrives home from his trip, what do you think he will do to the farmhands?"

"He'll kill them—a rotten bunch, and good riddance," they answered. "Then he'll assign the vineyard to farmhands who will hand over the profits when it's time."

Jesus said, "Right—and you can read it for yourselves in your Bibles:

> The stone the masons threw out
> > is now the cornerstone.
> This is God's work;
> > we rub our eyes, we can hardly believe it!

"This is the way it is with you. God's kingdom will be taken back from you and handed over to a people who will live out a kingdom life. Whoever stumbles on this Stone gets shattered; whoever the Stone falls on gets smashed."

When the religious leaders heard this story, they knew it was aimed at them.

See also Mark 12:1-12; Luke 20:9-19

VISIO DIVINA

PAUSE. Take a minute to recall what emerged in your lectio meditation with this parable and stay with it as you pray with this drawing, *Stones*.

SEE. Search for all the pieces: an oblique angle, an oblique ancient tale, and an oblique prophetic metaphor; a stone tower, a stone wall, the throwing of stones, the stone that was rejected, and the chosen cornerstone.

PONDER. As you ponder the power in Jesus' "tell it slant" approach with his opposition, what do you wonder? How does the imagery of stones build an argument that the religious leaders begin to understand is pointed at them?

PRAY. Allow the authority, strength, and wisdom of Jesus to draw you into a posture of prayer and praise.

REFLECT. When Jesus is killed, as the parable foretells, what looks like total rejection and defeat becomes the very means for true life and wholeness for those who believe. As you prayerfully reflect on the words "This is God's work; we rub our eyes, we can hardly believe it!" (Matthew 21:42), turn your eyes once more to the rejected stone in the drawing.

LIVE. How do the harshness, the brokenness, the sacrifice, and the redemption of this story move you to live differently in response?

STONES

16

THE WEDDING BANQUET

Matthew 22:1-14

. . . .

In the Temple courts in Jerusalem, Jesus is once again addressing the chief priests and Pharisees, this time with a powerful parable of preparation for entering the Kingdom of Heaven. It's a tumultuous time for Jesus, who is in his final week of earthly life and ministry. This happens just after his triumphal entrance into Jerusalem and before his crucifixion.

SIMILE. The Kingdom of Heaven is like a king who prepares a wedding banquet for his son. Those who are invited refuse to join the festivities. Even with knowledge of the banquet feast of prime rib, they mistreat the servants and pay no attention, keeping on with their lives. This enrages the king.

CONTRAST. God's invitation to the Kingdom of Heaven, exemplified by the glorious wedding banquet of his beloved son, is offered to all. The king's generosity to the righteous and faithful is diametrically opposed to the Jewish leaders and others who want nothing to do with Jesus. In lieu of a wedding feast, they are tied up and shipped to hell!

LECTIO DIVINA

PAUSE. Sit silently and reverently with the Lord and invite him to make his presence known to you during this prayerfully reflective experience.

READ. Read the parable of Jesus a few times, either silently or aloud. Begin to notice what words and/or phrases pop off the page and land in your heart.

PONDER. Meditate on the parable, lingering with each word on the page. Note what's being formed in your heart and mind around the meaning of the parable.

PRAY. Formulate a prayer based on what you're noticing in the parable. Pay particular attention to the prompting of the Spirit toward one aspect of the parable.

REFLECT. Hold the parable like a diamond or a prism, looking at it from as many angles as possible. Notice any nuance or texture to the parable that feels invitational.

LIVE. Incarnate the truth you've discovered for your life today. Ask the Lord if there is one aspect of today's parable that you need to emulate in your sphere of influence. Or simply receive the parable as a gift for your soul.

THE WEDDING BANQUET

Matthew 22:1-14

Jesus responded by telling still more stories. "God's kingdom," he said, "is like a king who threw a wedding banquet for his son. He sent out servants to call in all the invited guests. And they wouldn't come!

"He sent out another round of servants, instructing them to tell the guests, 'Look, everything is on the table, the prime rib is ready for carving. Come to the feast!'

"They only shrugged their shoulders and went off, one to weed his garden, another to work in his shop. The rest, with nothing better to do, beat up on the messengers and then killed them. The king was outraged and sent his soldiers to destroy those thugs and level their city.

"Then he told his servants, 'We have a wedding banquet all prepared but no guests. The ones I invited weren't up to it. Go out into the busiest intersections in town and invite anyone you find to the banquet.' The servants went out on the streets and rounded up everyone they laid eyes on, good and bad, regardless. And so the banquet was on—every place filled.

"When the king entered and looked over the scene, he spotted a man who wasn't properly dressed. He said to him, 'Friend, how dare you come in here looking like that!' The man was speechless. Then the king told his servants, 'Get him out of here—fast. Tie him up and ship him to hell. And make sure he doesn't get back in.'

"That's what I mean when I say, 'Many get invited; only a few make it.'"

VISIO DIVINA

· · · · · · · · ·

PAUSE. Recenter your thoughts upon Jesus as you pray with this drawing, *The Wedding Banquet.*

SEE. Gaze upon this scene with your imagination. Where do you see hints of royalty, extravagance, and generosity? What else would you include to complete the setting?

PONDER. Continue to imagine this wedding feast in your mind's eye. As you envision yourself in attendance, what wedding clothes would you desire to put on to reflect how your heart is toward Jesus?

PRAY. Ask Jesus about what he desires for you to put off and put on as you come daily to the Kingdom table set before you.

REFLECT. How have you experienced generosity? What is it like to be offered the generosity of grace and belonging at the table of the Lord?

LIVE. How would life be different if you said a wholehearted, resolute "YES!" to God's hospitality?

THE WEDDING BANQUET

17

THE FIG TREE

Matthew 24:32-35; Mark 13:28-31; Luke 21:29-33

. . . .

On the Mount of Olives, Jesus is speaking to his disciples about the signs of the times and the coming of the Kingdom of God. He's being straightforward with them about his second coming and the end of the age. This is difficult for them to comprehend. He says, "Sky and earth will wear out; my words won't wear out" (Matthew 24:35).

SIMILE. The fig tree, and all other trees, display signs of the times, symbolic of the ushering in of the Kingdom of God. As the leaves on a tree sprout in summer, so, too, has the Kingdom drawn near. Jesus' departure from the disciples' presence is coming soon. They will need to stay alert to the signs. His time is imminent and palpable.

CONTRAST. The green blossoms of the summer season presume forthcoming seasons. Here we are introduced to God's eternal calendar. The fig tree's budding leaves are indicative of a new season coming very soon. Therefore, be aware, vigilant, and ready. The discernment of visible signs will lead to the assurance of the invisible.

LECTIO DIVINA

• • • • • • • • •

PAUSE. Sit silently and reverently with the Lord and invite him to make his presence known to you during this prayerfully reflective experience.

READ. Read the parable of Jesus a few times, either silently or aloud. Begin to notice what words and/or phrases pop off the page and land in your heart.

PONDER. Meditate on the parable, lingering with each word on the page. Note what's being formed in your heart and mind around the meaning of the parable.

PRAY. Formulate a prayer based on what you're noticing in the parable. Pay particular attention to the prompting of the Spirit toward one aspect of the parable.

REFLECT. Hold the parable like a diamond or a prism, looking at it from as many angles as possible. Notice any nuance or texture to the parable that feels invitational.

LIVE. Incarnate the truth you've discovered for your life today. Ask the Lord if there is one aspect of today's parable that you need to emulate in your sphere of influence. Or simply receive the parable as a gift for your soul.

THE FIG TREE
Matthew 24:32-35

"Take a lesson from the fig tree. From the moment you notice its buds form, the merest hint of green, you know summer's just around the corner. So it is with you: When you see all these things, you'll know he's at the door. Don't take this lightly. I'm not just saying this for some future generation, but for all of you. This age continues until all these things take place. Sky and earth will wear out; my words won't wear out."

See also Mark 13:28-31; Luke 21:29-33

VISIO DIVINA

PAUSE. Continuing to pray with this parable, ask God for his perspective as you sit with this drawing, *The Fig Tree*.

SEE. Examine the signs of new growth on the fig tree. Can you imagine the delicate, green tints of the infant leaf unfolding at the end of its twig? How many different shades of green can you imagine as this tree welcomes the new growing season?

PONDER. What growing seasons do you experience in the place where you live? Can you think of sights or smells that evoke a sense of change in the air? Is there a particular plant or tree that you watch carefully to observe the coming of a new season?

PRAY. Are there seasons of health, seasons of work, seasons of relationship, or seasons of prayer that are in a state of change in your life right now? Come to the Lord in what you are noticing and share your heart with him.

REFLECT. How do you want to become more watchful and aware of the times? How do you want to become more hopeful with readiness for the new life that God promises to bring about?

LIVE. Consider today what would nurture readiness and hopefulness. Lean into it.

THE FIG TREE

18

THE TEN VIRGINS

Matthew 25:1-13

• • • • • • • • •

The Mount of Olives, just across the Kidron Valley from Jerusalem, offers a panoramic view of the city. It's a place of biblical significance at crucial moments in Jesus' ministry: his triumphal entry, delivering the Olivet discourse (Matthew 24–25), the garden of Gethsemane (at the base of the mountain), and after his resurrection.

SIMILE. Ten young virgins, oil lamps in hand, await the arrival of the bridegroom. Five are silly and bring their lamps without extra oil. Five are smart and make sure to bring additional oil for their lamps. When the bridegroom doesn't appear as expected, they all fall asleep. In the middle of the night he arrives, ready for their greeting.

CONTRAST. Five smart and five silly virgins awaiting the bridegroom's arrival. Plentiful oil and no oil. Prepared and unprepared. Vigilance and laziness. Inside the wedding feast and locked outside. The ten virgins give us a clear picture of awaiting the fullness of the Kingdom of Heaven. Open to all who are ready; closed to those who lack purposeful preparation.

LECTIO DIVINA

PAUSE. Sit silently and reverently with the Lord and invite him to make his presence known to you during this prayerfully reflective experience.

READ. Read the parable of Jesus a few times, either silently or aloud. Begin to notice what words and/or phrases pop off the page and land in your heart.

PONDER. Meditate on the parable, lingering with each word on the page. Note what's being formed in your heart and mind around the meaning of the parable.

PRAY. Formulate a prayer based on what you're noticing in the parable. Pay particular attention to the prompting of the Spirit toward one aspect of the parable.

REFLECT. Hold the parable like a diamond or a prism, looking at it from as many angles as possible. Notice any nuance or texture to the parable that feels invitational.

LIVE. Incarnate the truth you've discovered for your life today. Ask the Lord if there is one aspect of today's parable that you need to emulate in your sphere of influence. Or simply receive the parable as a gift for your soul.

THE TEN VIRGINS

Matthew 25:1-13

"God's kingdom is like ten young virgins who took oil lamps and went out to greet the bridegroom. Five were silly and five were smart. The silly virgins took lamps, but no extra oil. The smart virgins took jars of oil to feed their lamps. The bridegroom didn't show up when they expected him, and they all fell asleep.

"In the middle of the night someone yelled out, 'He's here! The bridegroom's here! Go out and greet him!'

"The ten virgins got up and got their lamps ready. The silly virgins said to the smart ones, 'Our lamps are going out; lend us some of your oil.'

"They answered, 'There might not be enough to go around; go buy your own.'

"They did, but while they were out buying oil, the bridegroom arrived. When everyone who was there to greet him had gone into the wedding feast, the door was locked.

"Much later, the other virgins, the silly ones, showed up and knocked on the door, saying, 'Master, we're here. Let us in.'

"He answered, 'Do I know you? I don't think I know you.'

"So stay alert. You have no idea when he might arrive."

VISIO DIVINA

• • • • • • • • •

PAUSE. Recall the thoughts, emotions, or questions that were evoked while reading this parable and stay with them as you pray with this visual, *Meeting the Bridegroom*.

SEE. What is your eye drawn to as you scan the whole scene? Remain with that part of the image in a posture of prayerful openness. After you have given enough time to linger there, scan the entire image again. Notice the light in the darkness, the movement, and the stillness. What do you wonder? What do you desire?

PONDER. Consider the themes of longing and affection as you ponder this parable. What do you love, and what do you long for? If it were promised that your love and your longing would one day meet, what tireless diligence would you undergo to make sure you were ready?

PRAY. Take what you are noticing to Jesus in prayer. Be still with him for a while.

REFLECT. What emerged in your time of prayerfulness? Return to the image *Meeting the Bridegroom*, and put yourself in the scene. Allow yourself to wonder about your relationship with the One who is coming again.

LIVE. Do you sense an invitation to live differently?

MEETING THE BRIDEGROOM

19

THE TALENTS/MINAS

Matthew 25:14-30; Luke 19:11-27

. . . .

Jesus is continuing his Olivet discourse, on the Mount of Olives, with his disciples after experiencing his triumphal entry and before suffering his crucifixion. In this second of three consecutive parables, Jesus is telling them a story about stewardship, faithfulness, fruitfulness, and accountability—a reminder of our ultimate reckoning.

SIMILE. A man is planning to go on a long, extended journey. Before commencing his travels, he calls his servants together and entrusts his wealth to them while he's away. To one he gives five thousand dollars, to another two thousand, to a third one thousand. The man dispenses according to ability, holding each to account for their stewardship.

CONTRAST. The first two servants are made partners with the master. The third is thrown out into darkness. The first two multiply their money wisely. The third takes it upon himself to judge the master, hide his money, and give it back unchanged. The master is delighted with the first two and damns the third, who risked the least.

LECTIO DIVINA

PAUSE. Sit silently and reverently with the Lord and invite him to make his presence known to you during this prayerfully reflective experience.

READ. Read the parable of Jesus a few times, either silently or aloud. Begin to notice what words and/or phrases pop off the page and land in your heart.

PONDER. Meditate on the parable, lingering with each word on the page. Note what's being formed in your heart and mind around the meaning of the parable.

PRAY. Formulate a prayer based on what you're noticing in the parable. Pay particular attention to the prompting of the Spirit toward one aspect of the parable.

REFLECT. Hold the parable like a diamond or a prism, looking at it from as many angles as possible. Notice any nuance or texture to the parable that feels invitational.

LIVE. Incarnate the truth you've discovered for your life today. Ask the Lord if there is one aspect of today's parable that you need to emulate in your sphere of influence. Or simply receive the parable as a gift for your soul.

THE TALENTS/MINAS

Matthew 25:14-30

"It's also like a man going off on an extended trip. He called his servants together and delegated responsibilities. To one he gave five thousand dollars, to another two thousand, to a third one thousand, depending on their abilities. Then he left. Right off, the first servant went to work and doubled his master's investment. The second did the same. But the man with the single thousand dug a hole and carefully buried his master's money.

"After a long absence, the master of those three servants came back and settled up with them. The one given five thousand dollars showed him how he had doubled his investment. His master commended him: 'Good work! You did your job well. From now on be my partner.'

"The servant with the two thousand showed how he also had doubled his master's investment. His master commended him: 'Good work! You did your job well. From now on be my partner.'

"The servant given one thousand said, 'Master, I know you have high standards and hate careless ways, that you demand the best and make no allowances for error. I was afraid I might disappoint you, so I found a good hiding place and secured your money. Here it is, safe and sound down to the last cent.'

"The master was furious. 'That's a terrible way to live! It's criminal to live cautiously like that! If you knew I was after the best, why did you do less than the least? The least you could have done would have been to invest the sum with the bankers, where at least I would have gotten a little interest.

"'Take the thousand and give it to the one who risked the most. And get rid of this "play-it-safe" who won't go out on a limb. Throw him out into utter darkness.'"

See also Luke 19:11-27

VISIO DIVINA

PAUSE. Making time to be attentive, welcome the presence of God's Spirit as you contemplate this piece of artwork, *Going out on a Limb*.

SEE. Study the carefully positioned and skillfully steadied hands in this drawing until you can visually discern what is about to happen in this game of marbles. Imagine the focus, the expectancy, the risk, and the intentionality of the moment. Will the servant be able to strike and claim another marble for the master? How do the jars of marbles presented on the master's table illustrate the story Jesus tells about stewarding God's gifts? What do you see?

PONDER. How does it feel to put yourself out there, sharing your resources and using your gifts? What is it like to take risks, to let go of your grasp on things, and to shed pride in hopes of fruitfulness for the Kingdom of God?

PRAY. Spend some time with God today, prayerfully reflecting on what gifts and resources he has given you. In a spirit of confession, talk to him about your level of trust in taking risks. What do you want to ask God for?

REFLECT. Return to the image of marbles, and think about one marble—one gift or resource God has given you that needs to be given away or practiced.

LIVE. Focusing on one marble at a time, how do you hope to trust God as you steward what he has given you?

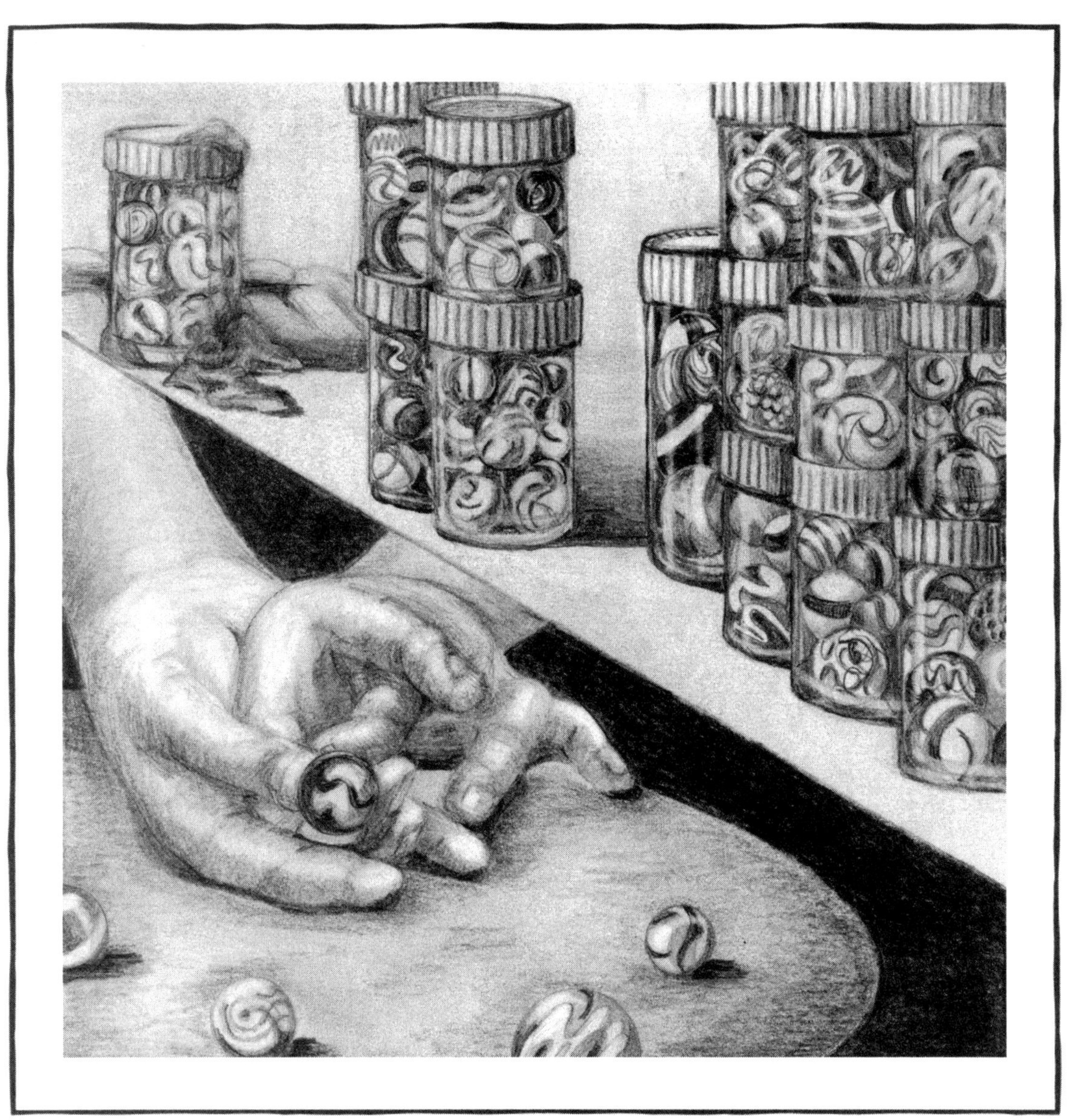

GOING OUT ON A LIMB

20

THE SHEEP AND THE GOATS

Matthew 25:31-46

. . . .

This is the third parable in the Olivet discourse. Jesus is teaching about the end times and the final judgment. As the nations are gathered in front of the Son of Man, he will separate them from one another according to their faithfulness. The sheep will receive their rightful inheritance; the goats he will usher away due to what they have done or left undone.

SIMILE. As a good shepherd sorts out the sheep from the goats, God himself will call all to account when the Son of Man comes again in glory. On the right are the sheep, who are blessed by the Father and invited to receive their inheritance. On the left are the goats, who are cast into the fires of hell for their hardness of heart.

CONTRAST. The sheep are full of compassion and mercy, and this delights the King. Their willingness to feed the hungry, replenish the thirsty, care for the homeless, clothe the poor, and visit the sick and imprisoned pleases the Lord. The goats see the same needs and ignore them. That displeases the King. What is done to others (or not) is done to God.

LECTIO DIVINA

PAUSE. Sit silently and reverently with the Lord and invite him to make his presence known to you during this prayerfully reflective experience.

READ. Read the parable of Jesus a few times, either silently or aloud. Begin to notice what words and/or phrases pop off the page and land in your heart.

PONDER. Meditate on the parable, lingering with each word on the page. Note what's being formed in your heart and mind around the meaning of the parable.

PRAY. Formulate a prayer based on what you're noticing in the parable. Pay particular attention to the prompting of the Spirit toward one aspect of the parable.

REFLECT. Hold the parable like a diamond or a prism, looking at it from as many angles as possible. Notice any nuance or texture to the parable that feels invitational.

LIVE. Incarnate the truth you've discovered for your life today. Ask the Lord if there is one aspect of today's parable that you need to emulate in your sphere of influence. Or simply receive the parable as a gift for your soul.

THE SHEEP AND THE GOATS

Matthew 25:31-46

"When he finally arrives, blazing in beauty and all his angels with him, the Son of Man will take his place on his glorious throne. Then all the nations will be arranged before him and he will sort the people out, much as a shepherd sorts out sheep and goats, putting sheep to his right and goats to his left.

"Then the King will say to those on his right, 'Enter, you who are blessed by my Father! Take what's coming to you in this kingdom. It's been ready for you since the world's foundation. And here's why:

> I was hungry and you fed me,
> I was thirsty and you gave me a drink,
> I was homeless and you gave me a room,
> I was shivering and you gave me clothes,
> I was sick and you stopped to visit,
> I was in prison and you came to me.'

"Then those 'sheep' are going to say, 'Master, what are you talking about? When did we ever see you hungry and feed you, thirsty and give you a drink? And when did we ever see you sick or in prison and come to you?' Then the King will say, 'I'm telling the solemn truth: Whenever you did one of these things to someone overlooked or ignored, that was me—you did it to me.'

"Then he will turn to the 'goats,' the ones on his left, and say, 'Get out, worthless goats! You're good for nothing but the fires of hell. And why? Because—

> I was hungry and you gave me no meal,
> I was thirsty and you gave me no drink,
> I was homeless and you gave me no bed,
> I was shivering and you gave me no clothes,
> Sick and in prison, and you never visited.'

"Then those 'goats' are going to say, 'Master, what are you talking about? When did we ever see you hungry or thirsty or homeless or shivering or sick or in prison and didn't help?'

"He will answer them, 'I'm telling the solemn truth: Whenever you failed to do one of these things to someone who was being overlooked or ignored, that was me— you failed to do it to me.'"

"Then those 'goats' will be herded to their eternal doom, but the 'sheep' to their eternal reward."

PAUSE. Simply rest a moment with the Lord, remembering what stood out to you in this parable. Stay with it as you pray with this drawing, *Unto Me*.

SEE. Slowly and prayerfully, take a visual journey around the borders of the drawing, connecting with the needs of the overlooked and the ignored. Contemplate the parable's personification of the sheep and the goat as you gaze into their eyes and into their hearts.

PONDER. Can you see yourself in the sheep or the goat? Or both?

PRAY. Talk to the Lord about what is stirring in you as you consider this parable.

REFLECT. What is it like for you to consider Jesus' words "Whenever you did one of these things to someone overlooked or ignored, that was me—you did it to me" (Matthew 25:40) or "Whenever you failed to do one of these things to someone overlooked or ignored, that was me, you failed to do it to me" (Matthew 25:45)?

LIVE. With God's help, what concrete change would you like to make in your life going forward?

UNTO ME

THE GROWING SEED

Mark 4:26-29

. . . .

This parable is unique to the Gospel of Mark but similar in nature to others Jesus articulated using basic agricultural imagery. Addressing those who are gathered along the Sea of Galilee, he takes every possible opportunity to teach life-giving truth to the large crowds. He also takes time to explain the meaning of each story to his disciples.

SIMILE. The Kingdom of God is like seed scattered in a field by a man, presumably a farmer. It's thrown indiscriminately and left alone to take root, sprout, and grow on its own. The seed produces a stem, then a bud, and then ripened grain. When it's ripe and ready to harvest, the farmer—thanks to God—harvests a healthy crop.

CONTRAST. The work of God's Kingdom includes both the efforts of humans and the invisible work of God. The farmer plants the seeds and harvests the crop. The Spirit takes the scattered seeds and brings forth a fruitful harvest. The human, earthly efforts of the farmer are combined with the hidden, glorious, under-the-surface growth of each seed.

LECTIO DIVINA

PAUSE. Sit silently and reverently with the Lord and invite him to make his presence known to you during this prayerfully reflective experience.

READ. Read the parable of Jesus a few times, either silently or aloud. Begin to notice what words and/or phrases pop off the page and land in your heart.

PONDER. Meditate on the parable, lingering with each word on the page. Note what's being formed in your heart and mind around the meaning of the parable.

PRAY. Formulate a prayer based on what you're noticing in the parable. Pay particular attention to the prompting of the Spirit toward one aspect of the parable.

REFLECT. Hold the parable like a diamond or a prism, looking at it from as many angles as possible. Notice any nuance or texture to the parable that feels invitational.

LIVE. Incarnate the truth you've discovered for your life today. Ask the Lord if there is one aspect of today's parable that you need to emulate in your sphere of influence. Or simply receive the parable as a gift for your soul.

THE GROWING SEED

Mark 4:26-29

Then Jesus said, "God's kingdom is like seed thrown on a field by a man who then goes to bed and forgets about it. The seed sprouts and grows— he has no idea how it happens. The earth does it all without his help: first a green stem of grass, then a bud, then the ripened grain. When the grain is fully formed, he reaps—harvest time!"

<h1 style="text-align:center">VISIO DIVINA</h1>

• • • • • • • • •

PAUSE. Remain in a prayerful posture as you focus on this drawing, *The Growing Seed*.

SEE. Let your eye trace the story of the growing seed around the perimeters of the artwork. Notice the farmer's two contrasting postures and their significance or insignificance to the seed's story. Where do the farmer's story and the seed's story intersect?

PONDER. What surprises you about this parable? Do you experience resonance or dissonance with this simile of the Kingdom of God? Why?

PRAY. Bring what you are experiencing into the light of Jesus and let his presence minister to you as you pray.

REFLECT. How is Jesus inviting you to partner with God in the work of his Kingdom? What is that like for you?

When does he make it clear to hold back on your *doing* and just be restful, trusting that he is at work? What is that like for you?

LIVE. How do you want to live into a trusting and faithful life of work and rest with God?

THE GROWING SEED

22

THE CREDITOR AND
THE TWO DEBTORS

Luke 7:41-47

. . . .

Simon the Pharisee has invited Jesus to come to his home for a meal, most likely to trick Jesus or corner him—it certainly isn't to honor or please him. No customary expressions of basic hospitality are offered—no water for his feet, no greeting, nothing for freshening up—and yet Jesus graciously reclines at Simon's table.

SIMILE. A sinful woman stands at Jesus' feet, kissing them and pouring out expensive perfume salted with her tears. Jesus tells Simon a story of a creditor and two debtors. The Kingdom of Heaven is likened to the actions of the generous creditor to both one who owed much and one who owed little. His forgiveness is extravagant.

CONTRAST. This parable is filled with contrast. Simon the Pharisee and the sinful woman at the feet of Jesus. No customary hospitality by Simon yet freely offered by the woman. Two debtors and two distinct amounts owed to the creditor. Sinfulness upended by salvation. Judgment swallowed up by grace. Repentance's reward—the freedom of forgiveness. Compassion, goodness, and grace open the door to the Kingdom of God.

LECTIO DIVINA

PAUSE. Sit silently and reverently with the Lord and invite him to make his presence known to you during this prayerfully reflective experience.

READ. Read the parable of Jesus a few times, either silently or aloud. Begin to notice what words and/or phrases pop off the page and land in your heart.

PONDER. Meditate on the parable, lingering with each word on the page. Note what's being formed in your heart and mind around the meaning of the parable.

PRAY. Formulate a prayer based on what you're noticing in the parable. Pay particular attention to the prompting of the Spirit toward one aspect of the parable.

REFLECT. Hold the parable like a diamond or a prism, looking at it from as many angles as possible. Notice any nuance or texture to the parable that feels invitational.

LIVE. Incarnate the truth you've discovered for your life today. Ask the Lord if there is one aspect of today's parable that you need to emulate in your sphere of influence. Or simply receive the parable as a gift for your soul.

THE CREDITOR AND THE TWO DEBTORS

Luke 7:41-47

"Two men were in debt to a banker. One owed five hundred silver pieces, the other fifty. Neither of them could pay up, and so the banker canceled both debts. Which of the two would be more grateful?"

Simon answered, "I suppose the one who was forgiven the most."

"That's right," said Jesus. Then turning to the woman, but speaking to Simon, he said, "Do you see this woman? I came to your home; you provided no water for my feet, but she rained tears on my feet and dried them with her hair. You gave me no greeting, but from the time I arrived she hasn't quit kissing my feet. You provided nothing for freshening up, but she has soothed my feet with perfume. Impressive, isn't it? She was forgiven many, many sins, and so she is very, very grateful. If the forgiveness is minimal, the gratitude is minimal."

<h1 style="text-align:center">VISIO DIVINA</h1>

• • • • • • • •

PAUSE. Ask the Lord to open the eyes of your heart as you pray with this drawing, *Seen*.

SEE. Let your eyes move over and under all the intimate details of this visual interpretation. As you aim to really *see* the woman, recall Jesus' question of Simon: "Do you see this woman?" (Luke 7:44). What about you? What do you notice about this woman?

PONDER. What goes on inside you as you ponder Jesus' acknowledgment of this woman? What do you wonder about the connection between being forgiven and showing gratitude? Being seen and responding with affection?

PRAY. Simply quiet yourself before the Lord. Try closing your eyes to notice what is in your mind's eye. Draw near to God for several moments, and allow yourself to be seen.

REFLECT. What emerged in the quiet of your prayer? Gaze upon the artwork once more. Linger there, considering how deeply beholden you are to God.

LIVE. Does the volume of your gratitude proportionately line up with the greatness of your indebtedness? What response resides on the tip of your heart?

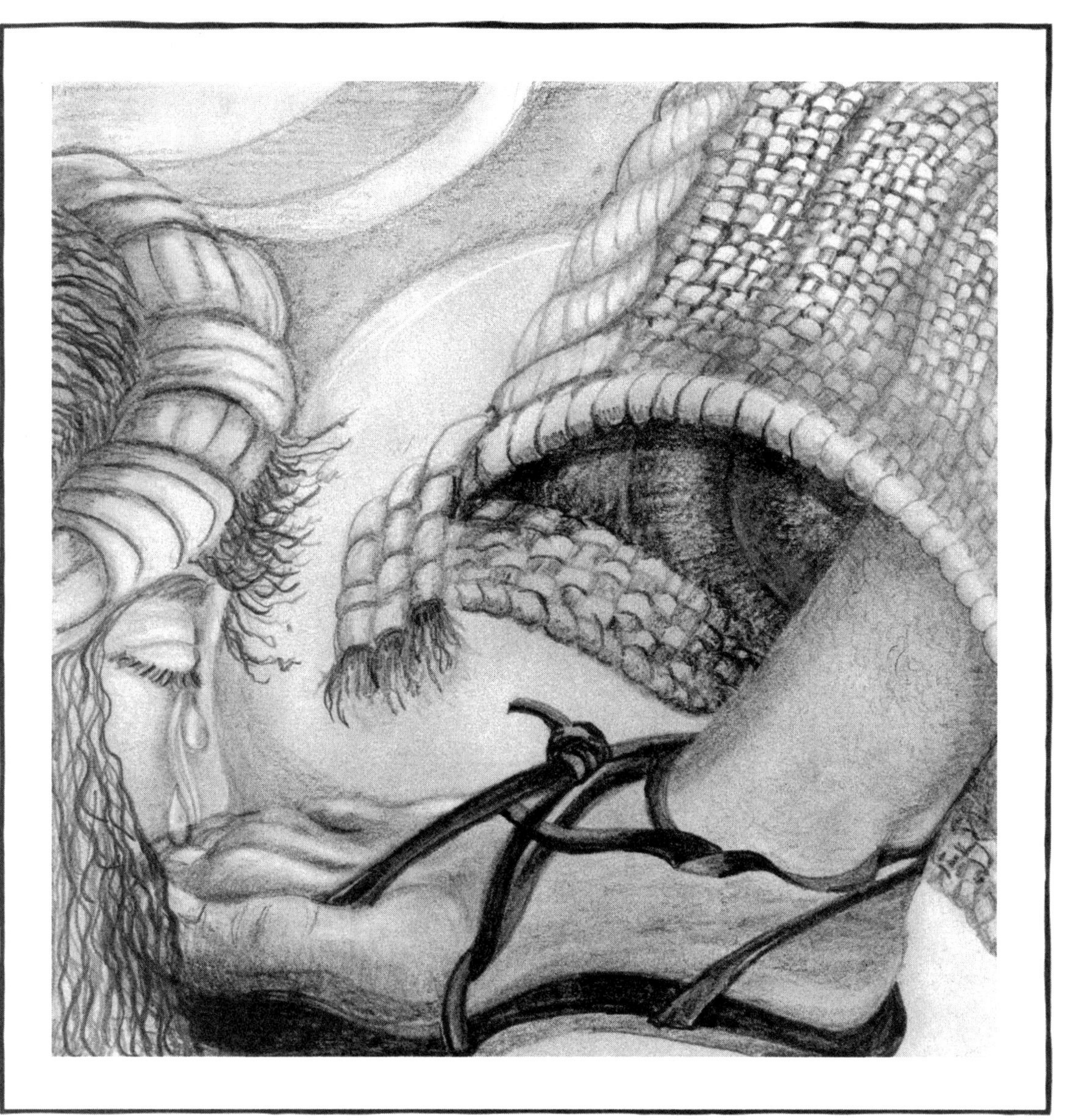

SEEN

23

THE SOWER

Matthew 13:1-9, 18-23; Mark 4:1-9; Luke 8:4-15

· · · · · · · · ·

In Matthew and Mark, we find Jesus along the shoreline of the Sea of Galilee, addressing a large crowd that has formed. He uses a boat as his pulpit and teaches one of our most beloved parables. In Luke, we travel with Jesus from town to town as he proclaims the Good News of the Kingdom of God to a large crowd eager to hear more.

SIMILE. Agricultural illustrations are frequent during Jesus' ministry years. Here we see the main ingredients for growing healthy crops: a sower, his seed, and the soil in which the seed is planted. It's here that Jesus speaks of four soils, three of which are less receptive and one that's ready for growth. The Kingdom abounds in good soil.

CONTRAST. The seeds on the road represent hearing the message, being unable to grasp it, and the evil one plucking it away. The seeds in the gravel stand for those who receive the Word with joy but have no root to sustain it. The seed that falls in the weeds references those who hear but for whom the worries and deceitfulness of wealth choke out the message. The seed in the good earth is indeed the most fruitful. A parable of the soul: seed sown by the Sower into the soil of the soul.

LECTIO DIVINA

PAUSE. Sit silently and reverently with the Lord and invite him to make his presence known to you during this prayerfully reflective experience.

READ. Read the parable of Jesus a few times, either silently or aloud. Begin to notice what words and/or phrases pop off the page and land in your heart.

PONDER. Meditate on the parable, lingering with each word on the page. Note what's being formed in your heart and mind around the meaning of the parable.

PRAY. Formulate a prayer based on what you're noticing in the parable. Pay particular attention to the prompting of the Spirit toward one aspect of the parable.

REFLECT. Hold the parable like a diamond or a prism, looking at it from as many angles as possible. Notice any nuance or texture to the parable that feels invitational.

LIVE. Incarnate the truth you've discovered for your life today. Ask the Lord if there is one aspect of today's parable that you need to emulate in your sphere of influence. Or simply receive the parable as a gift for your soul.

THE SOWER

Luke 8:4-15

As they went from town to town, a lot of people joined in and traveled along. He addressed them, using this story: "A farmer went out to sow his seed. Some of it fell on the road; it was tramped down and the birds ate it. Other seed fell in the gravel; it sprouted, but withered because it didn't have good roots. Other seed fell in the weeds; the weeds grew with it and strangled it. Other seed fell in rich earth and produced a bumper crop.

"Are you listening to this? Really listening?"

His disciples asked, "Why did you tell this story?"

He said, "You've been given insight into God's kingdom—you know how it works. There are others who need stories. But even with stories some of them aren't going to get it:

> Their eyes are open but don't see a thing,
> Their ears are open but don't hear a thing.

"This story is about some of those people. The seed is the Word of God. The seeds on the road are those who hear the Word, but no sooner do they hear it than the Devil snatches it from them so they won't believe and be saved.

"The seeds in the gravel are those who hear with enthusiasm, but the enthusiasm doesn't go very deep. It's only another fad, and the moment there's trouble it's gone.

"And the seed that fell in the weeds—well, these are the ones who hear, but then the seed is crowded out and nothing comes of it as they go about their lives worrying about tomorrow, making money, and having fun.

"But the seed in the good earth—these are the good-hearts who seize the Word and hold on no matter what, sticking with it until there's a harvest."

See also Matthew 13:1-9, 18-23; Mark 4:1-9

VISIO DIVINA

PAUSE. Ask the Lord to give you eyes that see and ears that hear as you sit with this drawing, *Soil Samples.*

SEE. Let your eyes examine each of the soil samples. Compare and contrast what you see with an inspector's eye. How is the intentionality of examining with a discerning eye different from a giving a quick glance? What are you finding?

PONDER. How is this kind of seeing much like the intentionality of listening with a discerning ear? What would it take to listen long and deep to God's Word?

PRAY. Be still with the Lord and take note of what comes up for you.

REFLECT. If you were to take a soil sample of the condition of your heart toward the Word of God, what might you discern?

LIVE. In what ways do you want to be the good earth with a heart that seizes the Word and holds on until there's a fruitful harvest?

SOIL SAMPLES

24

THE GOOD SAMARITAN

Luke 10:30-37

. . . .

A religion scholar stands up to test Jesus: "Teacher, what do I need to do to get eternal life?" (Luke 10:25). Jesus responds, "What's written in God's Law? How do you interpret it?" (Luke 10:26). The scholar answers correctly: "That you love the Lord your God with all your passion and prayer and muscle and intelligence—and that you love your neighbor as well as you do yourself" (Luke 10:27). But he struggles with how to do so.

SIMILE. For all here on earth who live in the Kingdom of God, the mandate is twofold: Love God with everything you are and have and love your neighbor as yourself. Jesus tells the story of a man who is attacked while walking from Jerusalem to Jericho. A priest and a Levite pass him by, but a Samaritan takes pity on him and rescues him from his plight.

CONTRAST. Being a neighbor has nothing to do with what's easy or convenient. Instead, it means releasing prejudice, embodying compassion, and extending God-honoring grace and kindness. This is seen in the tangible and tender mercy of the Samaritan, who bandages up the man's wounds, carries him to safety, provides means for his welfare, and follows up thereafter.

LECTIO DIVINA

PAUSE. Sit silently and reverently with the Lord and invite him to make his presence known to you during this prayerfully reflective experience.

READ. Read the parable of Jesus a few times, either silently or aloud. Begin to notice what words and/or phrases pop off the page and land in your heart.

PONDER. Meditate on the parable, lingering with each word on the page. Note what's being formed in your heart and mind around the meaning of the parable.

PRAY. Formulate a prayer based on what you're noticing in the parable. Pay particular attention to the prompting of the Spirit toward one aspect of the parable.

REFLECT. Hold the parable like a diamond or a prism, looking at it from as many angles as possible. Notice any nuance or texture to the parable that feels invitational.

LIVE. Incarnate the truth you've discovered for your life today. Ask the Lord if there is one aspect of today's parable that you need to emulate in your sphere of influence. Or simply receive the parable as a gift for your soul.

THE GOOD SAMARITAN

Luke 10:30-37

Jesus answered by telling a story. "There was once a man traveling from Jerusalem to Jericho. On the way he was attacked by robbers. They took his clothes, beat him up, and went off leaving him half-dead. Luckily, a priest was on his way down the same road, but when he saw him he angled across to the other side. Then a Levite religious man showed up; he also avoided the injured man.

"A Samaritan traveling the road came on him. When he saw the man's condition, his heart went out to him. He gave him first aid, disinfecting and bandaging his wounds. Then he lifted him onto his donkey, led him to an inn, and made him comfortable. In the morning he took out two silver coins and gave them to the innkeeper, saying, 'Take good care of him. If it costs any more, put it on my bill—I'll pay you on my way back.'

"What do you think? Which of the three became a neighbor to the man attacked by robbers?"

"The one who treated him kindly," the religion scholar responded.

Jesus said, "Go and do the same."

VISIO DIVINA

* * * * * * * * *

PAUSE. Ask God's Spirit to move inside your heart and mind as you consider this drawing, *The Good Samaritan.*

SEE. Allow your awareness to be renewed as you engage with a different perspective on what may be a familiar story. Put yourself in the place of the one who is robbed and attacked. As you look at this view: What do you feel in your body? What do you feel in your soul? What little can you see? What do you hear? What do you smell or even taste?

PONDER. Continue to ponder this rescue mission from the robbed man's perspective. What is it like to be at the mercy of an enemy who has become your neighbor? What is it like for your legs to give out on you so that you have to be loaded, face to fur, onto a donkey? What if the healing bed you are carried to resides in the camp of the despised? Who is your neighbor then? What else do you wonder about this rescue?

PRAY. Take a prayer walk with Jesus through your city or town, holding the question *Who is my neighbor?*

REFLECT. What God-awareness or self-awareness emerged during your prayer walk? Where do you need courage and compassion from God to live a life of being a neighbor, even with those who are difficult, inconvenient, or expensive to love?

LIVE. What next step toward compassion is the Lord inviting you to take this day?

THE GOOD SAMARITAN

25

THE FRIEND IN NEED

Luke 11:5-13

. . . .

Jesus delights in teaching his disciples about prayer. This parable is set within a larger teaching on prayer, including the Lord's Prayer (Luke 11:1-4) and further encouragement to ask, seek, and knock (Luke 11:9-13). Urgency, boldness, and persistence in prayer are highlighted in this desperate midnight interaction between two friends.

SIMILE. Prayer is central to our life in the Kingdom of God. In this parable, a friend is knocking on another friend's door in the middle of the night. He's seeking three loaves of bread to feed a friend who has shown up on his doorstep unannounced. The friend who is knocking does so continuously and fervently. He is on a mission fueled by his prayer.

CONTRAST. A formidable contrast in this parable is between the friend in bed, not wanting to be disturbed, and God, who doesn't see our prayers as a nuisance. It's not affection that motivates the friend to eventually get out of bed but the shameless audacity of the one who knocks and pleads earnestly for his help. Bold persistence energizes prayer.

163

LECTIO DIVINA

PAUSE. Sit silently and reverently with the Lord and invite him to make his presence known to you during this prayerfully reflective experience.

READ. Read the parable of Jesus a few times, either silently or aloud. Begin to notice what words and/or phrases pop off the page and land in your heart.

PONDER. Meditate on the parable, lingering with each word on the page. Note what's being formed in your heart and mind around the meaning of the parable.

PRAY. Formulate a prayer based on what you're noticing in the parable. Pay particular attention to the prompting of the Spirit toward one aspect of the parable.

REFLECT. Hold the parable like a diamond or a prism, looking at it from as many angles as possible. Notice any nuance or texture to the parable that feels invitational.

LIVE. Incarnate the truth you've discovered for your life today. Ask the Lord if there is one aspect of today's parable that you need to emulate in your sphere of influence. Or simply receive the parable as a gift for your soul.

THE FRIEND IN NEED

Luke 11:5-13

Then he said, "Imagine what would happen if you went to a friend in the middle of the night and said, 'Friend, lend me three loaves of bread. An old friend traveling through just showed up, and I don't have a thing on hand.'

"The friend answers from his bed, 'Don't bother me. The door's locked; my children are all down for the night; I can't get up to give you anything.'

"But let me tell you, even if he won't get up because he's a friend, if you stand your ground, knocking and waking all the neighbors, he'll finally get up and get you whatever you need.

"Here's what I'm saying:

Ask and you'll get;
Seek and you'll find;
Knock and the door will open.

"Don't bargain with God. Be direct. Ask for what you need. This is not a cat-and-mouse, hide-and-seek game we're in. If your little boy asks for a serving of fish, do you scare him with a live snake on his plate? If your little girl asks for an egg, do you trick her with a spider? As bad as you are, you wouldn't think of such a thing—you're at least decent to your own children. And don't you think the Father who conceived you in love will give the Holy Spirit when you ask him?"

VISIO DIVINA

PAUSE. Lean on Jesus to guide you as you pray with this image, *Knock*.

SEE. Take time to observe the texture in the drawing, noting that visual texture is created with the repetition of small lines and shapes as well as the repetition of dark and light values.

PONDER. This is a story of repetition. Regardless of the resistance, the friend in need is persistent in his request and continues his knocking until his neighbor relents and meets his need. How is prayer like knocking? How is prayer creating the very texture of faith and trust in God's attentiveness?

PRAY. Take a moment to prayerfully look at the hands God fashioned for you. Yes, look at your own hands and notice the texture and the repetition in the way they were formed. Hold your hands in a prayerful posture and thank God for his invitation to come to the door and knock.

REFLECT. How is your spiritual formation in Christ full of repetition and texture? What is Jesus showing you about repetition, perseverance, and patience in his relationship with you? What has been your awareness—has Christ been knocking at your door or you at his?

LIVE. Let your hands be a living, bodily reminder to never cease in offering the repetition and texture of continuous, prayerful knocking.

KNOCK

26

THE RICH FOOL

Luke 12:13-21

· · · · · · · · ·

A person in the crowd asks Jesus to intervene in a family inheritance matter. Jesus inquires in response, "Mister, what makes you think it's any of my business to be a judge or mediator for you?" (Luke 12:14). Jesus warns the people to watch their lives and guard their hearts against all kinds of greed. Life does not consist in an abundance of earthly possessions. Our riches are in God alone.

SIMILE. Life in the Kingdom of Heaven is filled with riches that come from the generous hand of the almighty God. The foolishness of those who think otherwise and pursue the accumulation of excessive riches on earth will eventuate in astonishment at the end of their lives. Greed for more cash, possessions, pleasures, and prestige will lead to a dead end.

CONTRAST. The dangers of greed and the true meaning of life confront one another in this straightforward parable. To pursue greed is to highlight the folly of earthly possessions. To focus on wealth and the hoarding of our belongings is to beckon relational destruction, both with one another and with God. Protect your heart from being captured by greed.

LECTIO DIVINA

PAUSE. Sit silently and reverently with the Lord and invite him to make his presence known to you during this prayerfully reflective experience.

READ. Read the parable of Jesus a few times, either silently or aloud. Begin to notice what words and/or phrases pop off the page and land in your heart.

PONDER. Meditate on the parable, lingering with each word on the page. Note what's being formed in your heart and mind around the meaning of the parable.

PRAY. Formulate a prayer based on what you're noticing in the parable. Pay particular attention to the prompting of the Spirit toward one aspect of the parable.

REFLECT. Hold the parable like a diamond or a prism, looking at it from as many angles as possible. Notice any nuance or texture to the parable that feels invitational.

LIVE. Incarnate the truth you've discovered for your life today. Ask the Lord if there is one aspect of today's parable that you need to emulate in your sphere of influence. Or simply receive the parable as a gift for your soul.

THE RICH FOOL

Luke 12:13-21

Someone out of the crowd said, "Teacher, order my brother to give me a fair share of the family inheritance."

He replied, "Mister, what makes you think it's any of my business to be a judge or mediator for you?"

Speaking to the people, he went on, "Take care! Protect yourself against the least bit of greed. Life is not defined by what you have, even when you have a lot."

Then he told them this story: "The farm of a certain rich man produced a terrific crop. He talked to himself: 'What can I do? My barn isn't big enough for this harvest.' Then he said, 'Here's what I'll do: I'll tear down my barns and build bigger ones. Then I'll gather in all my grain and goods, and I'll say to myself, Self, you've done well! You've got it made and can now retire. Take it easy and have the time of your life!'

"Just then God showed up and said, 'Fool! Tonight you die. And your barnful of goods—who gets it?'

"That's what happens when you fill your barn with Self and not with God."

VISIO DIVINA

PAUSE. Take a moment, trusting God to further unfold the passage as you pray with this image, *Many Barns.*

SEE. Enter this scene with your imagination. What do you imagine these barns are filled with? Notice the construction and design of these giant storehouses and imagine all the effort and labor involved in building and filling them. Notice the land beyond and all the possibilities for more.

PONDER. More! What in your life always holds possibilities for more? How much effort and thought do you put into having more of something? What do you like to have an extra supply of, just in case? What do you have plenty of and yet not enough to share or give away?

PRAY. Listen to the Lord and talk with him about what you are noticing about how much you value things.

REFLECT. Glance again at the drawing and prayerfully reflect, *What would it look like to fill my barns with more of God and less of me?*

LIVE. What is Jesus putting on your heart about desiring more of him?

MANY BARNS

27

THE WATCHFUL SERVANTS

Mark 13:32-37; Luke 12:35-40

The story of the watchful servants (Luke 12:35-40) is combined with that of the absent homeowner (Mark 13:32-37). They are similar but unique parables found in two synoptic Gospel locations. Each distinct pericope gives Jesus the opportunity to stress to his disciples the necessity of being ready for his eventual return. This story is part of a larger discourse on preparedness for Jesus' second coming.

SIMILE. The image of servants awaiting the return of their master from his honeymoon speaks of the unexpected hour when the Son of Man will arrive. If ready when he knocks on the door, they can immediately open it for him. Even if it's in the middle of the night or when the rooster crows at dawn. Today: Keep the lights on.

CONTRAST. Ready or not. Faithful or not. Watchful or not. These are the words of vigilance (or not) that Jesus is seeking to instill in the hearts and minds of his disciples. He is preparing them for his pending departure, urging them to remain faithful no matter what enemies seek to deter them. A promised reward awaits all who are prepared.

175

LECTIO DIVINA

PAUSE. Sit silently and reverently with the Lord and invite him to make his presence known to you during this prayerfully reflective experience.

READ. Read the parable of Jesus a few times, either silently or aloud. Begin to notice what words and/or phrases pop off the page and land in your heart.

PONDER. Meditate on the parable, lingering with each word on the page. Note what's being formed in your heart and mind around the meaning of the parable.

PRAY. Formulate a prayer based on what you're noticing in the parable. Pay particular attention to the prompting of the Spirit toward one aspect of the parable.

REFLECT. Hold the parable like a diamond or a prism, looking at it from as many angles as possible. Notice any nuance or texture to the parable that feels invitational.

LIVE. Incarnate the truth you've discovered for your life today. Ask the Lord if there is one aspect of today's parable that you need to emulate in your sphere of influence. Or simply receive the parable as a gift for your soul.

THE WATCHFUL SERVANTS

Luke 12:35-40

"Keep your shirts on; keep the lights on! Be like house servants waiting for their master to come back from his honeymoon, awake and ready to open the door when he arrives and knocks. Lucky the servants whom the master finds on watch! He'll put on an apron, sit them at the table, and serve them a meal, sharing his wedding feast with them. It doesn't matter what time of the night he arrives; they're awake—and so blessed!

"You know that if the house owner had known what night the burglar was coming, he wouldn't have stayed out late and left the place unlocked. So don't you be lazy and careless. Just when you don't expect him, the Son of Man will show up."

See also Mark 13:32-37

VISIO DIVINA

PAUSE. Open your heart to Jesus as you pray with this drawing, *Waiting*.

SEE. What catches your eye as you survey this room? What does the youthfulness and simplicity of the scene evoke in you? Notice if a memory, an emotion, or a question arises.

PONDER. What happens in the waiting? What are the gifts given to your inmost being in times of watching? What do you want to tell the child in you about the importance of watchful hope?

PRAY. Create a space for God and invite him to fill it. Try to form a simple breath prayer: breathing out a longing, breathing in a truth.

REFLECT. What aspects of this parable speak into your life right now?

LIVE. How might your prayers be different if you chose to wait for the Lord, fully awake, with your lights on?

WAITING

28

THE FAITHFUL AND WISE SERVANT

Matthew 24:45-51; Luke 12:42-48

. . . .

The faithful and wise servant parable is a continuation of Jesus' teaching on the importance of the disciples' readiness for his subsequent return. It is part of his wider discourse on both the certainty of his coming again and the importance of living faithfully now. Again in this story, the servant doesn't know the time the master will return.

SIMILE. The Kingdom of God is filled with friends of God who are diligent in all aspects of their daily life stewardship. To know God is to show it with faithfulness and obedience. Jesus warns against complacency and against exploitation of our God-given authority. Being self-indulgent, neglectful, or nasty to others is a stench in the nostrils of a loving God.

CONTRAST. A servant who consistently knows and does the master's will is diametrically opposed to one who disregards the master and is therefore deserving of harsh punishment. The accountability and consequences of disobedience are astonishing. Great gifts mean great responsibilities; greater gifts mean even greater responsibilities.

LECTIO DIVINA

• • • • • • • • •

PAUSE. Sit silently and reverently with the Lord and invite him to make his presence known to you during this prayerfully reflective experience.

READ. Read the parable of Jesus a few times, either silently or aloud. Begin to notice what words and/or phrases pop off the page and land in your heart.

PONDER. Meditate on the parable, lingering with each word on the page. Note what's being formed in your heart and mind around the meaning of the parable.

PRAY. Formulate a prayer based on what you're noticing in the parable. Pay particular attention to the prompting of the Spirit toward one aspect of the parable.

REFLECT. Hold the parable like a diamond or a prism, looking at it from as many angles as possible. Notice any nuance or texture to the parable that feels invitational.

LIVE. Incarnate the truth you've discovered for your life today. Ask the Lord if there is one aspect of today's parable that you need to emulate in your sphere of influence. Or simply receive the parable as a gift for your soul.

THE FAITHFUL AND WISE SERVANT
Luke 12:42-48

The Master said, "Let me ask you: Who is the dependable manager, full of common sense, that the master puts in charge of his staff to feed them well and on time? He is a blessed man if when the master shows up he's doing his job. But if he says to himself, 'The master is certainly taking his time,' begins beating up on the servants and maids, throws parties for his friends, and gets drunk, the master will walk in when he least expects it, give him the thrashing of his life, and put him back in the kitchen peeling potatoes.

"The servant who knows what his master wants and ignores it, or insolently does whatever he pleases, will be thoroughly thrashed. But if he does a poor job through ignorance, he'll get off with a slap on the hand. Great gifts mean great responsibilities; greater gifts, greater responsibilities!"

See also Matthew 24:45-51

VISIO DIVINA

• • • • • • • • •

PAUSE. Remember the Lord's presence with you as you pray with this drawing, *Feeding the Workers.*

SEE. Follow the oblique angle of the ladle in the drawing. What is being connected?

Notice the posture of the hand that is serving. What manner does it suggest to you?

What comes up for you as you look upon this depiction?

PONDER. What does it mean to be hungry, and what does it mean to be fed, both physically and spiritually? What manner and what environment enable effective feeding to take place in community?

PRAY. Talk to Jesus about your awareness of hunger and thirst in your body and soul.

REFLECT. Consider the community or lack of community that you are experiencing in this season of your life. What is your part in nurturing others? What is your experience of being fed?

LIVE. If you are to be found a faithful servant, as described in the parable, what might be an important next step to take in the context of community?

FEEDING THE WORKERS

29

THE BARREN TREE

Luke 13:6-9

• • • • • • • • •

Addressing both his disciples and a larger crowd that has gathered, Jesus is emphasizing a call to repentance in the simple story of the barren tree: "Unless you turn to God, you, too, will die" (Luke 13:5). This is nothing new for Jesus; he continually and patiently urges everyone to come to repentance and embrace his with-God Kingdom life.

SIMILE. The Kingdom of Heaven is likened to an apple tree in this parable. It is barren for years, yet the gardener defends the tree from the owner, who wishes to cut it down. The gardener proposes cultivating the soil and fertilizing the roots instead. The owner is appeased, the gardener is tasked, and the tree is given additional nourishment and time.

CONTRAST. The unfertilized tree is offered nourishment that will enliven its roots and bring forth fruitfulness. Though it was once barren, now there is hope for the tree's transformation. A patient gardener speaks up to the impulsive vineyard owner and saves the tree from immediate demise. The patient work of renewal gives time for the tree to bear lasting bounty.

LECTIO DIVINA

PAUSE. Sit silently and reverently with the Lord and invite him to make his presence known to you during this prayerfully reflective experience.

READ. Read the parable of Jesus a few times, either silently or aloud. Begin to notice what words and/or phrases pop off the page and land in your heart.

PONDER. Meditate on the parable, lingering with each word on the page. Note what's being formed in your heart and mind around the meaning of the parable.

PRAY. Formulate a prayer based on what you're noticing in the parable. Pay particular attention to the prompting of the Spirit toward one aspect of the parable.

REFLECT. Hold the parable like a diamond or a prism, looking at it from as many angles as possible. Notice any nuance or texture to the parable that feels invitational.

LIVE. Incarnate the truth you've discovered for your life today. Ask the Lord if there is one aspect of today's parable that you need to emulate in your sphere of influence. Or simply receive the parable as a gift for your soul.

THE BARREN TREE
Luke 13:6-9

Then he told them a story: "A man had an apple tree planted in his front yard. He came to it expecting to find apples, but there weren't any. He said to his gardener, 'What's going on here? For three years now I've come to this tree expecting apples and not one apple have I found. Chop it down! Why waste good ground with it any longer?'

"The gardener said, 'Let's give it another year. I'll dig around it and fertilize, and maybe it will produce next year; if it doesn't, then chop it down.'"

VISIO DIVINA

• • • • • • • • •

PAUSE. In a prayerful posture, open your heart to God's Spirit as you consider this drawing, *Mercy*.

SEE. Angles and diagonal lines can visually suggest action. Looking at the drawing, what action is being asserted upon the fruitless tree?

PONDER. Higher than other attributes, such as beauty or shade, bearing fruit makes an apple tree worth having. How often do you take stock of your fruitfulness?

PRAY. Take what you are noticing into a quiet place of self-examination with your loving heavenly Father.

REFLECT. How is the Gardener of your soul showing his mercy? How is he digging around you and fertilizing the soil of your soul for more fruitfulness? Are you receiving or resisting his cultivating care?

LIVE. How is this parable of second chances a gift for you today?

MERCY

30

THE PLACE OF HONOR

Luke 14:7-14

. . . .

Most of Luke 14 speaks to the importance of biblical hospitality. Here we see Jesus being entertained on the Sabbath by a prominent Pharisee. It's fascinating to listen in on Jesus' very direct teaching about the humble hospitality God prefers in his Kingdom. When invited to a feast, not only the great banquet of the Kingdom but in other settings as well, it's best to choose the humble, lowly seat.

SIMILE. The Kingdom of God is filled with those who practice loving generosity to the humble by the humble. Jesus illustrates this by giving voice to what he is noticing about this particular Sabbath table. If we self-select the last place first, we might in fact be invited to a seat of honor. Humility—and contentment—displace the need for privilege.

CONTRAST. Humility is the social custom of God's Kingdom. Jesus is masterful in reversing the pride of this world with the behaviors of his Kingdom. Enter with a humble and grateful heart, prefer others, serve the lowest and the least, and let God do the honoring he desires. "If you're content to be simply yourself, you will become more than yourself" (Luke 14:11).

LECTIO DIVINA

. . . .

PAUSE. Sit silently and reverently with the Lord and invite him to make his presence known to you during this prayerfully reflective experience.

READ. Read the parable of Jesus a few times, either silently or aloud. Begin to notice what words and/or phrases pop off the page and land in your heart.

PONDER. Meditate on the parable, lingering with each word on the page. Note what's being formed in your heart and mind around the meaning of the parable.

PRAY. Formulate a prayer based on what you're noticing in the parable. Pay particular attention to the prompting of the Spirit toward one aspect of the parable.

REFLECT. Hold the parable like a diamond or a prism, looking at it from as many angles as possible. Notice any nuance or texture to the parable that feels invitational.

LIVE. Incarnate the truth you've discovered for your life today. Ask the Lord if there is one aspect of today's parable that you need to emulate in your sphere of influence. Or simply receive the parable as a gift for your soul.

THE PLACE OF HONOR

Luke 14:7-14

He went on to tell a story to the guests around the table. Noticing how each had tried to elbow into the place of honor, he said, "When someone invites you to dinner, don't take the place of honor. Somebody more important than you might have been invited by the host. Then he'll come and call out in front of everybody, 'You're in the wrong place. The place of honor belongs to this man.' Embarrassed, you'll have to make your way to the very last table, the only place left.

"When you're invited to dinner, go and sit at the last place. Then when the host comes he may very well say, 'Friend, come up to the front.' That will give the dinner guests something to talk about! What I'm saying is, If you walk around all high and mighty, you're going to end up flat on your face. But if you're content to be simply yourself, you will become more than yourself."

Then he turned to the host. "The next time you put on a dinner, don't just invite your friends and family and rich neighbors, the kind of people who will return the favor. Invite some people who never get invited out, the misfits from the wrong side of the tracks. You'll be—and experience— a blessing. They won't be able to return the favor, but the favor will be returned—oh, how it will be returned!—at the resurrection of God's people."

VISIO DIVINA

PAUSE. As you make time to be attentive, welcome the Lord to be with you while you look at this drawing, *The Place of Honor.*

SEE. How does your eye move across the composition of this drawing? Where does your eye want to sit? Why?

PONDER. If these chairs could speak the voices of your culture, what would each one be saying to you? Prayerfully discern: Where is there invitation, and where is there temptation?

PRAY. Bring what you are noticing about humility to Jesus. Have a conversation with him.

REFLECT. How does this parable intersect with your life? How does it challenge or affirm choices that you make in your life?

LIVE. What is the Lord inviting you to be or to do in response?

THE PLACE OF HONOR

31

THE GREAT BANQUET

Luke 14:15-24

· · · · · · · · · ·

At the table of a prominent Pharisee, one of the guests remarks, "How fortunate the one who gets to eat dinner in God's kingdom!" (Luke 14:15). Typical for Jesus' approach to teaching about the Kingdom, he responds with a story: Many were invited to a great banquet, but when the banquet was ready, everyone had lame reasons for their absence.

SIMILE. To reject the summons to attend the banquet prepared for them would be considered anathema. Their excuses angered the host, and he sent his servant back out to the streets to quickly fill his table so they could feast. The religious leaders of Jesus' time wanted nothing to do with Jesus. They rejected his offer to join the banquet.

CONTRAST. There is urgency in Jesus' voice. The banquet of all banquets has been prepared. But there is widespread rejection. The self-absorbed and self-sufficient reject Jesus. The Kingdom of Heaven is for the humble—"the misfits and homeless and down-and-out" (Luke 14:21). God's Kingdom is for all who receive Jesus' generous hospitality.

LECTIO DIVINA

PAUSE. Sit silently and reverently with the Lord and invite him to make his presence known to you during this prayerfully reflective experience.

READ. Read the parable of Jesus a few times, either silently or aloud. Begin to notice what words and/or phrases pop off the page and land in your heart.

PONDER. Meditate on the parable, lingering with each word on the page. Note what's being formed in your heart and mind around the meaning of the parable.

PRAY. Formulate a prayer based on what you're noticing in the parable. Pay particular attention to the prompting of the Spirit toward one aspect of the parable.

REFLECT. Hold the parable like a diamond or a prism, looking at it from as many angles as possible. Notice any nuance or texture to the parable that feels invitational.

LIVE. Incarnate the truth you've discovered for your life today. Ask the Lord if there is one aspect of today's parable that you need to emulate in your sphere of influence. Or simply receive the parable as a gift for your soul.

THE GREAT BANQUET

Luke 14:15-24

That triggered a response from one of the guests: "How fortunate the one who gets to eat dinner in God's kingdom!"

Jesus followed up. "Yes. For there was once a man who threw a great dinner party and invited many. When it was time for dinner, he sent out his servant to the invited guests, saying, 'Come on in; the food's on the table.'

"Then they all began to beg off, one after another making excuses. The first said, 'I bought a piece of property and need to look it over. Send my regrets.'

"Another said, 'I just bought five teams of oxen, and I really need to check them out. Send my regrets.'

"And yet another said, 'I just got married and need to get home to my wife.'

"The servant went back and told the master what had happened. He was outraged and told the servant, 'Quickly, get out into the city streets and alleys. Collect all who look like they need a square meal, all the misfits and homeless and down-and-out you can lay your hands on, and bring them here.'

"The servant reported back, 'Master, I did what you commanded—and there's still room.'

"The master said, 'Then go to the country roads. Whoever you find, drag them in. I want my house full! Let me tell you, not one of those originally invited is going to get so much as a bite at my dinner party.'"

VISIO DIVINA

· · · · · · · · ·

PAUSE. Ask the Lord to continue to unfold the parable as you pray with this drawing, *Invited.*

SEE. Compare this depiction of the great banquet with the drawing *Wedding Feast* (page 113). What aspects of the Lord's feast are emphasized in each? How does this outdoor setting evoke a sense of welcome to all?

PONDER. Place yourself in the scene as one who has been invited. What goes on inside your heart and mind as you imagine the events of the night? Do you long to attend this banquet enough to drop everything else in order to have a seat at the table?

PRAY. Listen with the Lord and talk to him about how you are either desiring to be all-in or holding on to excuses. Or both.

REFLECT. Glance again at the drawing as you consider who gets a seat at the banquet. What challenges or questions arise in your heart and mind?

LIVE. As you allow this parable to rock your preconceived notions, how do you want God to enable you to change your behavior and your perspective?

INVITED

32

THE COST OF BEING A DISCIPLE

Luke 14:25-35

. . . .

As the crowds begin to swell, Jesus takes every opportunity to teach them about the centrality of the Kingdom of God and the cost of following him. He is always straightforward about the total surrender it requires. In this parable, he uses a handful of mini parables to put emphasis on the demanding nature of discipleship.

SIMILE. Here are several metaphorical examples of the main point Jesus is seeking to convey. First, he mentions the need to have greater affection for God than for one's father, mother, spouse, children, siblings, and even self. Second, he references a builder of an unfinished house. Then a king who is preparing for battle. Finally, remaining salty salt.

CONTRAST. Salt doesn't lose its ability to season or preserve on its own. But if it is exposed to water, the sodium chloride can dissolve and the essence of salt diluted. Salt can hold permanence, loyalty, durability, usefulness, and value. It has no expiration date. We are the "salt-seasoning that brings out the God-flavors of this earth" (Matthew 5:13).

LECTIO DIVINA

• • • • • • • • •

PAUSE. Sit silently and reverently with the Lord and invite him to make his presence known to you during this prayerfully reflective experience.

READ. Read the parable of Jesus a few times, either silently or aloud. Begin to notice what words and/or phrases pop off the page and land in your heart.

PONDER. Meditate on the parable, lingering with each word on the page. Note what's being formed in your heart and mind around the meaning of the parable.

PRAY. Formulate a prayer based on what you're noticing in the parable. Pay particular attention to the prompting of the Spirit toward one aspect of the parable.

REFLECT. Hold the parable like a diamond or a prism, looking at it from as many angles as possible. Notice any nuance or texture to the parable that feels invitational.

LIVE. Incarnate the truth you've discovered for your life today. Ask the Lord if there is one aspect of today's parable that you need to emulate in your sphere of influence. Or simply receive the parable as a gift for your soul.

THE COST OF BEING A DISCIPLE

Luke 14:25-35

One day when large groups of people were walking along with him, Jesus turned and told them, "Anyone who comes to me but refuses to let go of father, mother, spouse, children, brothers, sisters—yes, even one's own self!—can't be my disciple. Anyone who won't shoulder his own cross and follow behind me can't be my disciple.

"Is there anyone here who, planning to build a new house, doesn't first sit down and figure the cost so you'll know if you can complete it? If you only get the foundation laid and then run out of money, you're going to look pretty foolish. Everyone passing by will poke fun at you: 'He started something he couldn't finish.'

"Or can you imagine a king going into battle against another king without first deciding whether it is possible with his ten thousand troops to face the twenty thousand troops of the other? And if he decides he can't, won't he send an emissary and work out a truce?

"Simply put, if you're not willing to take what is dearest to you, whether plans or people, and kiss it good-bye, you can't be my disciple.

"Salt is excellent. But if the salt goes flat, it's useless, good for nothing.

"Are you listening to this? Really listening?"

VISIO DIVINA

• • • • • • • • •

PAUSE. Continuing to pray with this parable, ask God for his perspective as you sit with this drawing, *Salt of the Earth*.

SEE. Zoom out on the big picture of a world groaning with pain. Then zoom in on the call to endure the pain and the cost of being the salt of the earth. What do you perceive as you pray with the artwork?

PONDER. What does it mean to be the salt that seasons and brings out the best of what life is meant to be? What does it mean to be a preservative, to safeguard love? How is that a costly call?

PRAY. Lean upon the mighty arms of God as you consider the cost of saltiness with him.

REFLECT. How is Jesus teaching you healthy ways to choose sacrifice, suffering, and surrender for the sake of love and faithfulness as his disciple?

Who inspires you as someone who has counted the cost and shouldered their cross as the salt of the earth for Christ? (Consider spending some time with their story as a way to further your prayer.)

LIVE. What costly next step is Jesus inviting you to take with him?

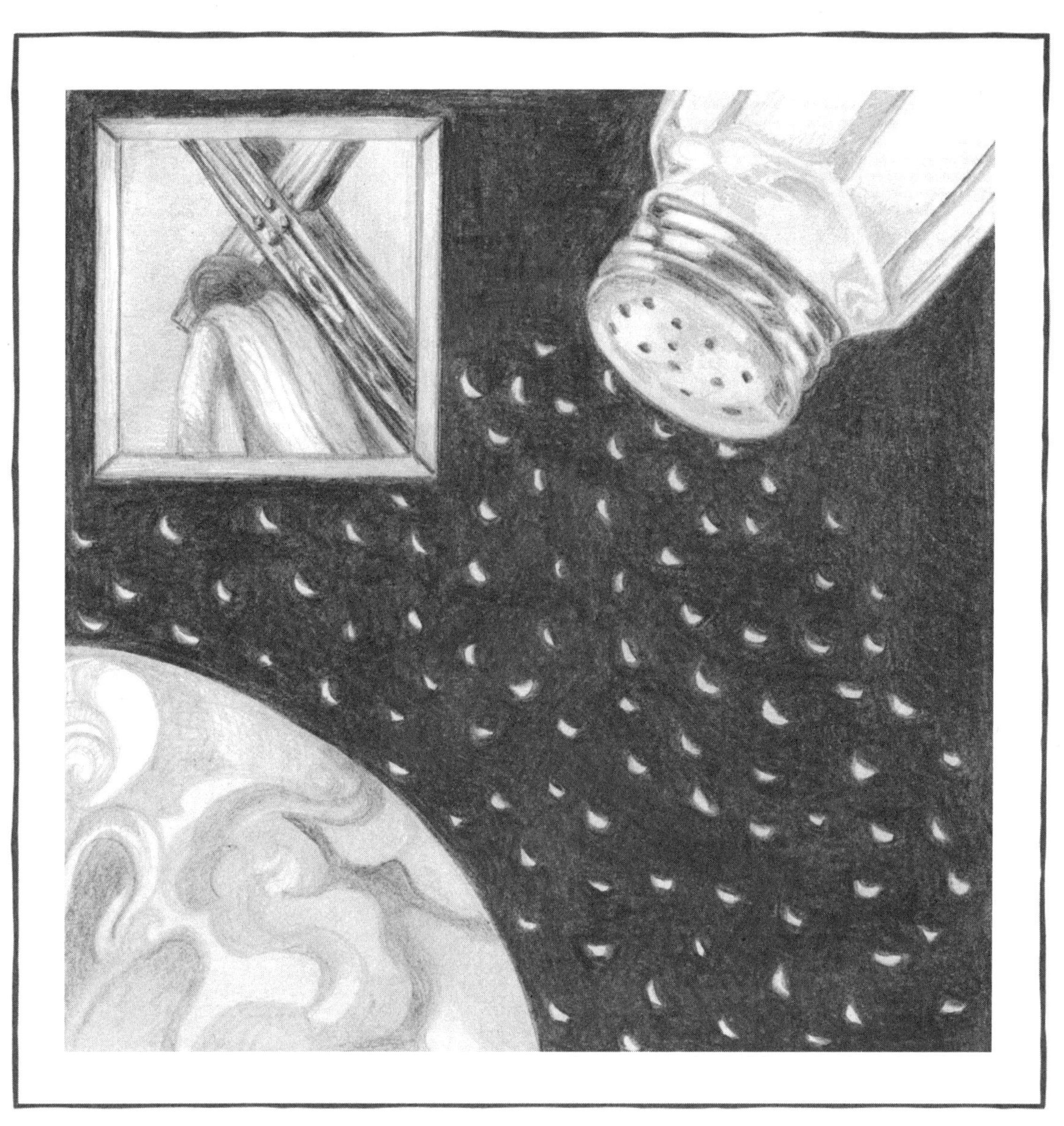

SALT OF THE EARTH

33

THE LOST SHEEP

Matthew 18:12-14; Luke 15:1-7

In this chapter of Matthew, Jesus is addressing his disciples, teaching them about the Kingdom of Heaven and urging them to focus on the care of the childlike and with loving humility to avoid causing them to stumble. In Luke's Gospel, Jesus is speaking directly to the Pharisees and religion scholars, who were critical of his association with sinners and people of questionable reputation.

SIMILE. Owning one hundred sheep carries with it a lot of responsibility. Every sheep in the fold matters. Therefore, when one of them is lost, the owner will do everything possible to search for the wayward and beckon it home. He leaves the ninety-nine, trusting they will be safe in the open field. When the lost sheep is found, everyone celebrates.

CONTRAST. Illustrative of God's love for every individual, this parable makes certain his unconditional affection for the lost, least, lonely, little, and left behind. These lost sheep are in contrast to the ninety-nine sheep who are already safely in the shepherd's watchful care. In addition, Jesus is rebuking the haughty attitude of the religious leaders, focusing instead on the boundless grace of God.

LECTIO DIVINA

PAUSE. Sit silently and reverently with the Lord and invite him to make his presence known to you during this prayerfully reflective experience.

READ. Read the parable of Jesus a few times, either silently or aloud. Begin to notice what words and/or phrases pop off the page and land in your heart.

PONDER. Meditate on the parable, lingering with each word on the page. Note what's being formed in your heart and mind around the meaning of the parable.

PRAY. Formulate a prayer based on what you're noticing in the parable. Pay particular attention to the prompting of the Spirit toward one aspect of the parable.

REFLECT. Hold the parable like a diamond or a prism, looking at it from as many angles as possible. Notice any nuance or texture to the parable that feels invitational.

LIVE. Incarnate the truth you've discovered for your life today. Ask the Lord if there is one aspect of today's parable that you need to emulate in your sphere of influence. Or simply receive the parable as a gift for your soul.

THE LOST SHEEP

Luke 15:1-7

By this time a lot of men and women of questionable reputation were hanging around Jesus, listening intently. The Pharisees and religion scholars were not pleased, not at all pleased. They growled, "He takes in sinners and eats meals with them, treating them like old friends." Their grumbling triggered this story.

"Suppose one of you had a hundred sheep and lost one. Wouldn't you leave the ninety-nine in the wilderness and go after the lost one until you found it? When found, you can be sure you would put it across your shoulders, rejoicing, and when you got home call in your friends and neighbors, saying, 'Celebrate with me! I've found my lost sheep!' Count on it—there's more joy in heaven over one sinner's rescued life than over ninety-nine good people in no need of rescue."

See also Matthew 18:12-14

PAUSE. Ask Jesus to help you know his love while you gaze upon the details of *The Lost Sheep*.

SEE. Notice the gradation of values as this scene takes you from a detailed, dark foreground to atmospherically lightened hills in the distance. How do both distance and perspective play a part in creating the tone of the story?

Linger with this landscape and all its details, noticing if there is a particular aspect that evokes a memory, a feeling, or a question within you.

PONDER. As you ponder this story, whom do you identify with? The lost sheep? The shepherd? The ninety-nine?

PRAY. Take whatever you are noticing with you into a quiet place of prayer. What do you want to tell Jesus right now? What do you sense he might want to tell you?

REFLECT. In what ways does the metaphor of the Good Shepherd inform your understanding of the character of God? How does this metaphor touch your own life in some way? (Consider reading Psalm 23 as part of your reflection.)

LIVE. What would change if you truly lived from a place of knowing your belovedness?

THE LOST SHEEP

34

THE LOST COIN

Luke 15:8-10

. . . .

The second in a trio of parables about loss, here we have the story of a woman who loses a coin. She's diligently searching for it, illustrative of Jesus' relentless pursuit of all who are spiritually lost. His primary audience here is the Pharisees and religion scholars, continual critics of him. They are constantly, obsessively irritated by him.

SIMILE. Like a woman who loses a coin and diligently searches for it, so is the heart of God toward any who are spiritually adrift. The persistence of the woman to find this coin speaks of Jesus' inherent reaching out for those who are lost, least, lonely, little, or left behind. This includes sinners and people of questionable reputation who find freedom and joy in Jesus' presence.

CONTRAST. Nine coins are secure but one is missing. Instead of simply ignoring the lost one, the woman launches a diligent search to seek and to find it, to rescue it from its lostness and welcome it home. So it is with the heart of God toward any who are not yet found. Jesus is in relentless pursuit to find and restore all who are rejected or lost.

LECTIO DIVINA

PAUSE. Sit silently and reverently with the Lord and invite him to make his presence known to you during this prayerfully reflective experience.

READ. Read the parable of Jesus a few times, either silently or aloud. Begin to notice what words and/or phrases pop off the page and land in your heart.

PONDER. Meditate on the parable, lingering with each word on the page. Note what's being formed in your heart and mind around the meaning of the parable.

PRAY. Formulate a prayer based on what you're noticing in the parable. Pay particular attention to the prompting of the Spirit toward one aspect of the parable.

REFLECT. Hold the parable like a diamond or a prism, looking at it from as many angles as possible. Notice any nuance or texture to the parable that feels invitational.

LIVE. Incarnate the truth you've discovered for your life today. Ask the Lord if there is one aspect of today's parable that you need to emulate in your sphere of influence. Or simply receive the parable as a gift for your soul.

THE LOST COIN

Luke 15:8-10

"Imagine a woman who has ten coins and loses one. Won't she light a lamp
and scour the house, looking in every nook and cranny until she finds it?
And when she finds it you can be sure she'll call her friends and neighbors:
'Celebrate with me! I found my lost coin!' Count on it—that's the kind of
party God's angels throw every time one lost soul turns to God."

VISIO DIVINA

PAUSE. Take a moment to put on a posture of holy curiosity as you look at this drawing, *Celebrate.*

SEE. How does the merriment depict a heavenly quality of joy? What moves in you as you notice the gestures of delight? What would you add to the scene to depict how you would celebrate your greatest joy?

PONDER. As you consider the heart of God rejoicing and all heaven celebrating over the one who is found, what are you curious about?

PRAY. Quiet yourself with Jesus, listening and reflecting on his deep love for the lost.

REFLECT. How does this parable connect with your life, your relationships, and your walk with God?

LIVE. Are you sensing an invitation from God? How does your heart want to respond?

CELEBRATE

THE PRODIGAL SON

Luke 15:11-24

． ． ． ． ． ． ． ．

One of the most profound and deeply moving parables of Jesus, this story focuses our attention on the radical, unconditional, and extravagant love of the Father. It's spoken in response to the criticism of the Pharisees and religion scholars, who are always upset by Jesus' welcoming affection for sinners who come to him to be found, forgiven, blessed, and restored.

SIMILE. We are immediately enveloped by this Kingdom story of grace. A man has two sons. The younger asks for and receives his share of the inheritance. He leaves home for a distant country, where he squanders his wealth on wasteful living. He is homeless, hungry, and hurting. Eating corncobs with the pigs, he finally comes to his senses and returns home.

CONTRAST. The younger son leaves home wealthy but soon becomes destitute—poor and needy. Sinfulness is only remedied by the father's forgiveness. Faithfulness is only experienced by continual grace. The prodigal gets lost in his journeys. But the brazen sinner is beautifully restored by the extravagant grace of his father's unconditional love.

LECTIO DIVINA

PAUSE. Sit silently and reverently with the Lord and invite him to make his presence known to you during this prayerfully reflective experience.

READ. Read the parable of Jesus a few times, either silently or aloud. Begin to notice what words and/or phrases pop off the page and land in your heart.

PONDER. Meditate on the parable, lingering with each word on the page. Note what's being formed in your heart and mind around the meaning of the parable.

PRAY. Formulate a prayer based on what you're noticing in the parable. Pay particular attention to the prompting of the Spirit toward one aspect of the parable.

REFLECT. Hold the parable like a diamond or a prism, looking at it from as many angles as possible. Notice any nuance or texture to the parable that feels invitational.

LIVE. Incarnate the truth you've discovered for your life today. Ask the Lord if there is one aspect of today's parable that you need to emulate in your sphere of influence. Or simply receive the parable as a gift for your soul.

THE PRODIGAL SON

Luke 15:11-24

Then he said, "There was once a man who had two sons. The younger said
to his father, 'Father, I want right now what's coming to me.'

"So the father divided the property between them. It wasn't long
before the younger son packed his bags and left for a distant country.
There, undisciplined and dissipated, he wasted everything he had. After
he had gone through all his money, there was a bad famine all through
that country and he began to feel it. He signed on with a citizen there who
assigned him to his fields to slop the pigs. He was so hungry he would
have eaten the corn-cobs in the pig slop, but no one would give him any.

"That brought him to his senses. He said, 'All those farmhands working
for my father sit down to three meals a day, and here I am starving to death.
I'm going back to my father. I'll say to him, Father, I've sinned against God,
I've sinned before you; I don't deserve to be called your son. Take me on as
a hired hand.' He got right up and went home to his father.

"When he was still a long way off, his father saw him. His heart
pounding, he ran out, embraced him, and kissed him. The son started his
speech: 'Father, I've sinned against God, I've sinned before you; I don't
deserve to be called your son ever again.'

"But the father wasn't listening. He was calling to the servants, 'Quick.
Bring a clean set of clothes and dress him. Put the family ring on his finger
and sandals on his feet. Then get a prize-winning heifer and roast it. We're
going to feast! We're going to have a wonderful time! My son is here—
given up for dead and now alive! Given up for lost and now found!' And
they began to have a wonderful time."

VISIO DIVINA

. . . .

PAUSE. Taking a deep breath, open yourself to the love of Jesus as you pray with this drawing, *Embrace*.

SEE. What captures your attention as you take in this scene? Allow your eyes to linger in places that evoke emotion, memories, or questions.

PONDER. What is God showing you about his character in this parable? What does coming home involve in the story?

PRAY. Find a quiet place to rest with Jesus, picturing yourself in his embrace.

REFLECT. Is there something about this story that connects to your story with God?

LIVE. In what ways do you long to come home to God? What would that mean for you today?

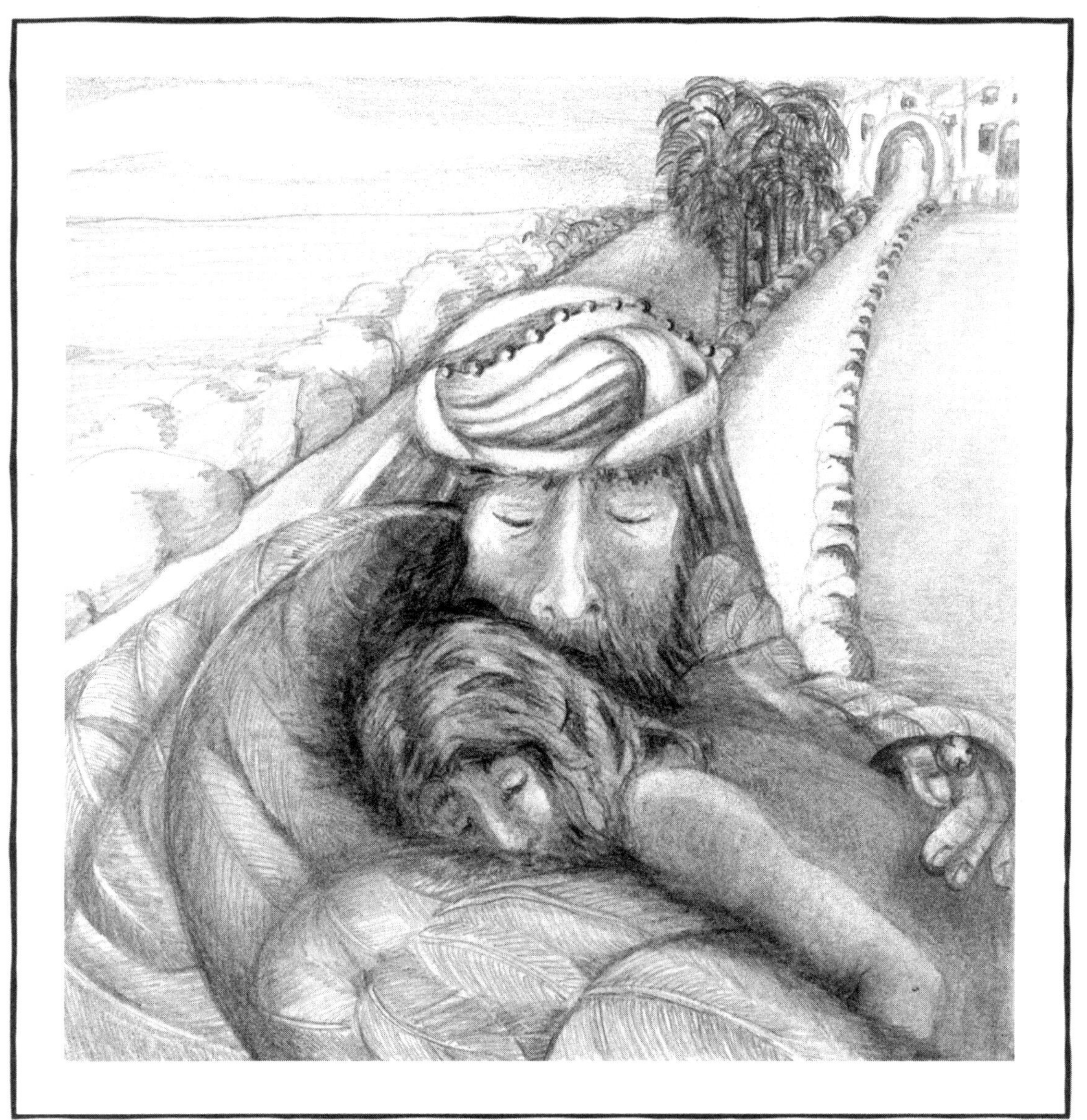

EMBRACE

THE OLDER SON

Luke 15:25-32

. . . .

Although the central character of this parable is the forgiving father, part two of the story is all about the response of his older son. Much to his chagrin, the older son discovers that his younger brother is now home after squandering his inheritance. Worse yet, there's a celebration in his honor. He's stunned, despondent, and angry.

SIMILE. The Kingdom of God is led by a Father who delights in welcoming home all who have been lost. From the porch of heaven, he waits for the repentant and is extravagant in his affectionate response. In the parable, this confuses and bewilders the older son, who has been a faithful worker in his father's business. His frustration arises from his dutiful existence.

CONTRAST. Both sons need heart transplants. The younger has come to his senses, but the older remains entrenched in his self-righteousness. Both sons get lost on their journeys even though the older son never leaves home. He is lost in his work, and his relationship with his father is broken. We are left hanging in limbo about the eventual choices of the older son. Will he ever accept his father's love?

LECTIO DIVINA

PAUSE. Sit silently and reverently with the Lord and invite him to make his presence known to you during this prayerfully reflective experience.

READ. Read the parable of Jesus a few times, either silently or aloud. Begin to notice what words and/or phrases pop off the page and land in your heart.

PONDER. Meditate on the parable, lingering with each word on the page. Note what's being formed in your heart and mind around the meaning of the parable.

PRAY. Formulate a prayer based on what you're noticing in the parable. Pay particular attention to the prompting of the Spirit toward one aspect of the parable.

REFLECT. Hold the parable like a diamond or a prism, looking at it from as many angles as possible. Notice any nuance or texture to the parable that feels invitational.

LIVE. Incarnate the truth you've discovered for your life today. Ask the Lord if there is one aspect of today's parable that you need to emulate in your sphere of influence. Or simply receive the parable as a gift for your soul.

THE OLDER SON

Luke 15:25-32

"All this time his older son was out in the field. When the day's work was
done he came in. As he approached the house, he heard the music and
dancing. Calling over one of the houseboys, he asked what was going on.
He told him, 'Your brother came home. Your father has ordered a feast—
barbecued beef!—because he has him home safe and sound.'

"The older brother stomped off in an angry sulk and refused to join in.
His father came out and tried to talk to him, but he wouldn't listen. The
son said, 'Look how many years I've stayed here serving you, never giving
you one moment of grief, but have you ever thrown a party for me and
my friends? Then this son of yours who has thrown away your money on
whores shows up and you go all out with a feast!'

"His father said, 'Son, you don't understand. You're with me all the
time, and everything that is mine is yours—but this is a wonderful time,
and we had to celebrate. This brother of yours was dead, and he's alive! He
was lost, and he's found!'"

VISIO DIVINA

· · · · · · · · ·

PAUSE. Ask the Holy Spirit to guide you as you pray with this drawing, *Resistance*.

SEE. Scan the whole scene. What details catch your attention? What creates the mood of the drawing?

Compare the two scenes *Embrace* (page 227) and *Resistance*. How do the contrasting settings of the open road and the shadows of the palm grove suggest something about heart condition?

PONDER. Imagine yourself there in the shadows of the palm grove. What do you hear? What do you wonder? What emotions arise in you? Notice if there are ways you identify with either the older son or the father as they converse.

PRAY. Take what you are noticing to the Lord in prayer.

REFLECT. Fix your gaze again on the father. How is the character of the father consistent throughout the whole story? How would you describe him?

What will the older son need to do or to be in order to fully come home to both his father and his brother?

LIVE. In what ways do you long to come home to God more fully? What would that mean for you today?

RESISTANCE

36

THE SHREWD MANAGER

Luke 16:1-13

. . . .

Jesus is speaking this difficult parable directly to his disciples, but most likely there are Jewish leaders listening too. At first glance, one might assume Jesus is promoting poor business dealings and unethical financial comportment. Instead, he is encouraging astute management practices and redemptive relationships with worldly counterparts.

SIMILE. The work of the Kingdom is compared to the shrewdness of a defiant manager. Fearing job loss, the manager is aware of his own limitations in finding other work. Ashamed to beg, he devises a plan. He invites all his master's debtors to come forward with what they owe and then tinkers with their debt. Surprisingly, the master commends his shrewd, streetwise crookedness. He knows the manager's heart.

CONTRAST. Jesus is noting the savvy way the crooked manager works the angles and maintains business relationships with the master's debtors. He's contrasting the shrewdness of the manager with the disciples' naïveté. To be streetwise for the Kingdom means that the disciples must use their wits and conspire for what is right and good.

LECTIO DIVINA

· · · · · · · · ·

PAUSE. Sit silently and reverently with the Lord and invite him to make his presence known to you during this prayerfully reflective experience.

READ. Read the parable of Jesus a few times, either silently or aloud. Begin to notice what words and/or phrases pop off the page and land in your heart.

PONDER. Meditate on the parable, lingering with each word on the page. Note what's being formed in your heart and mind around the meaning of the parable.

PRAY. Formulate a prayer based on what you're noticing in the parable. Pay particular attention to the prompting of the Spirit toward one aspect of the parable.

REFLECT. Hold the parable like a diamond or a prism, looking at it from as many angles as possible. Notice any nuance or texture to the parable that feels invitational.

LIVE. Incarnate the truth you've discovered for your life today. Ask the Lord if there is one aspect of today's parable that you need to emulate in your sphere of influence. Or simply receive the parable as a gift for your soul.

THE SHREWD MANAGER

Luke 16:1-13

Jesus said to his disciples, "There was once a rich man who had a manager. He got reports that the manager had been taking advantage of his position by running up huge personal expenses. So he called him in and said, 'What's this I hear about you? You're fired. And I want a complete audit of your books.'

"The manager said to himself, 'What am I going to do? I've lost my job as manager. I'm not strong enough for a laboring job, and I'm too proud to beg. . . . Ah, I've got a plan. Here's what I'll do . . . then when I'm turned out into the street, people will take me into their houses.'

"Then he went at it. One after another, he called in the people who were in debt to his master. He said to the first, 'How much do you owe my master?'

"He replied, 'A hundred jugs of olive oil.'

"The manager said, 'Here, take your bill, sit down here—quick now—write fifty.'

"To the next he said, 'And you, what do you owe?'

"He answered, 'A hundred sacks of wheat.'

"He said, 'Take your bill, write in eighty.'

"Now here's a surprise: The master praised the crooked manager! And why? Because he knew how to look after himself. Streetwise people are smarter in this regard than law-abiding citizens. They are on constant alert, looking for angles, surviving by their wits. I want you to be smart in the same way—but for what is *right*—using every adversity to stimulate you to creative survival, to concentrate your attention on the bare essentials, so you'll live, really live, and not complacently just get by on good behavior."

Jesus went on to make these comments:

> If you're honest in small things,
>> you'll be honest in big things;
> If you're a crook in small things,
>> you'll be a crook in big things.
> If you're not honest in small jobs,
>> who will put you in charge of the store?
> No worker can serve two bosses:
>> He'll either hate the first and love the second
> Or adore the first and despise the second.
>> You can't serve both God and the Bank.

VISIO DIVINA

· · · · · · · · ·

PAUSE. Ask the Lord for insight as you contemplate this drawing, *Navigating*.

SEE. Slow down with the details of the drawing. What do you notice about the two roads and Jesus' urging toward a more savvy approach to our lives and relationships? How does the higher road appear to be a more challenging road, requiring you to keep your wits about you? How does the lower road represent taking the easy way, requiring very little thought or effort? Could this scene in some way depict the sharp-witted choices needed for the with-God life?

PONDER. How does Jesus grab your attention with this unexpected story? Does it awaken you from complacent thinking? Life is full of forks in the road, requiring wise discernment as we navigate the relationships and the choices before us. How does being smart—for what is right in life and service—inspire you? How do the words "on constant alert, looking for angles, surviving by their wits" (Luke 16:8) invite you into prayerful and creative ways of building meaningful relationships for good?

PRAY. Turn your eyes upon Jesus in prayer. What is he offering you?

REFLECT. Look again at the drawing. What words would you put on the crossroad signs to represent your life and choices you are facing? Discern the difference between the two roads: the road of complacency and the road of creative survival, which leads to the higher ground of really living. How is God directing your life?

LIVE. What would it mean for you to trust God in the crossroads of life and be fully alert to his ways?

NAVIGATING

37

THE RICH MAN AND LAZARUS

Luke 16:19-31

. . . .

With full knowledge of the Pharisees' love of money (Luke 16:14), Jesus offers up this parable about wealth and responsibility. Their distorted and unbalanced financial view is instilled in their theology. Akin to those who espouse the prosperity gospel today, the Pharisees believed that wealth was a sign of God's favor upon them.

SIMILE. The Kingdom of Heaven is for those who listen to Moses and the prophets and who choose to follow Jesus in their lifetimes. For the beggar covered with sores, the choice is obvious. The rich man prefers a life of luxury. But when both men die, Lazarus is by the side of Abraham. Justice and judgment eventually come.

CONTRAST. The obvious distinction and disparity is between the rich man dressed in luxurious purple linen and the poor man covered with sores and living among dogs who lick his wounds. The more significant contrast is between the consolation of Lazarus in heaven and the torment of the rich man in hell. The chasm is big and eternal.

LECTIO DIVINA

PAUSE. Sit silently and reverently with the Lord and invite him to make his presence known to you during this prayerfully reflective experience.

READ. Read the parable of Jesus a few times, either silently or aloud. Begin to notice what words and/or phrases pop off the page and land in your heart.

PONDER. Meditate on the parable, lingering with each word on the page. Note what's being formed in your heart and mind around the meaning of the parable.

PRAY. Formulate a prayer based on what you're noticing in the parable. Pay particular attention to the prompting of the Spirit toward one aspect of the parable.

REFLECT. Hold the parable like a diamond or a prism, looking at it from as many angles as possible. Notice any nuance or texture to the parable that feels invitational.

LIVE. Incarnate the truth you've discovered for your life today. Ask the Lord if there is one aspect of today's parable that you need to emulate in your sphere of influence. Or simply receive the parable as a gift for your soul.

THE RICH MAN AND LAZARUS

Luke 16:19-31

"There once was a rich man, expensively dressed in the latest fashions, wasting his days in conspicuous consumption. A poor man named Lazarus, covered with sores, had been dumped on his doorstep. All he lived for was to get a meal from scraps off the rich man's table. His best friends were the dogs who came and licked his sores.

"Then he died, this poor man, and was taken up by the angels to the lap of Abraham. The rich man also died and was buried. In hell and in torment, he looked up and saw Abraham in the distance and Lazarus in his lap. He called out, 'Father Abraham, mercy! Have mercy! Send Lazarus to dip his finger in water to cool my tongue. I'm in agony in this fire.'

"But Abraham said, 'Child, remember that in your lifetime you got the good things and Lazarus the bad things. It's not like that here. Here he's consoled and you're tormented. Besides, in all these matters there is a huge chasm set between us so that no one can go from us to you even if he wanted to, nor can anyone cross over from you to us.'

"The rich man said, 'Then let me ask you, Father: Send him to the house of my father where I have five brothers, so he can tell them the score and warn them so they won't end up here in this place of torment.'

"Abraham answered, 'They have Moses and the Prophets to tell them the score. Let them listen to them.'

"'I know, Father Abraham,' he said, 'but they're not listening. If someone came back to them from the dead, they would change their ways.'

"Abraham replied, 'If they won't listen to Moses and the Prophets, they're not going to be convinced by someone who rises from the dead.'"

VISIO DIVINA

· · · · · · · · ·

PAUSE. Take a minute to recall what emerged in your lectio meditation with this parable, and stay with it as you pray with this drawing, *The Great Reversal.*

SEE. What makes the figures in the artwork appear fixed or stuck in their positions? Do you notice movement portrayed within the hourglass? How do you perceive the depiction of overall movement being applied to the subject matter in the artwork? What is about to happen?

PONDER. Muse upon the words "Here it is again, the Great Reversal: many of the first ending up last, and the last first" (Matthew 20:16). How does this statement apply to this parable as well?

PRAY. What do you need to say to Jesus? What is he saying to you?

REFLECT. When you reflect upon the imminent reality of the sands of time running out on both the rich and the poor, the powerful and the powerless, what stirs inside your heart and mind?

LIVE. How does this parable move you to live differently?

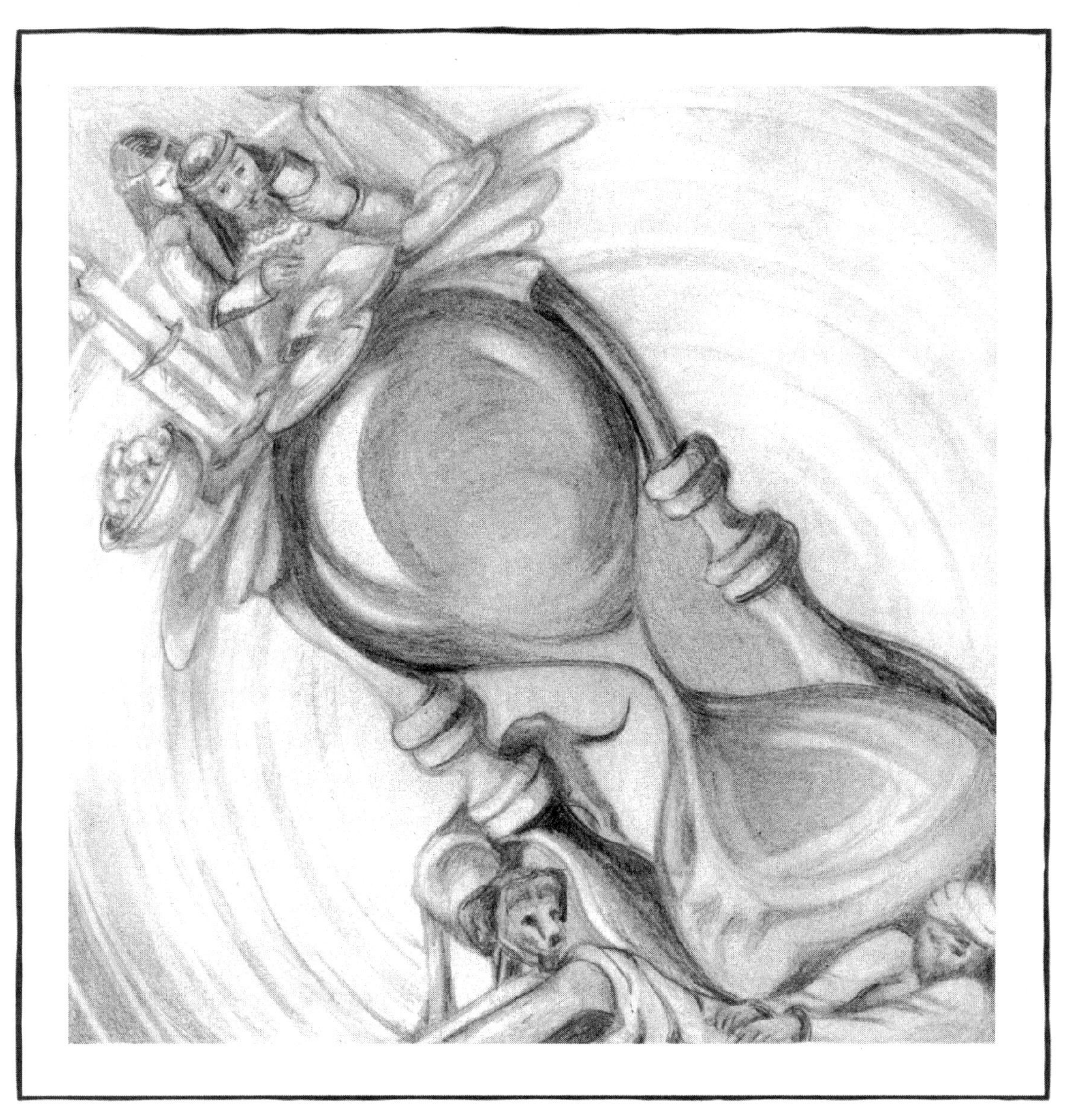

THE GREAT REVERSAL

38

THE OBEDIENT SERVANT

Luke 17:7-10

. . . .

Jesus is addressing his disciples here amid other teachings on sin, duty, and faith. If our sin causes another to stumble, it would be better for us to be thrown into the sea in a concrete vest. If your brother or sister sins against you, correct them, and if they repent, forgive them. And if you have faith the size of a poppy seed, you have power accessible from God.

SIMILE. According to Jesus, the Kingdom of Heaven is made up of those who willingly and obediently serve without making a big deal about their efforts. We do not serve God or others for the sake of their words of praise. We serve regardless of the response. We are not to act like entitled ones who demand or demean what a faithful life looks like for a child of God.

CONTRAST. Humility is to be the modus operandi for all disciples of Jesus. We are not to make a show of our daily faithfulness to the tasks at hand. Instead, we are to serve quietly, obediently, and consistently without any special attention, personal gain, or tangible reward. Our service is totally dependent upon God's generous goodness and all-sufficient grace.

LECTIO DIVINA

· · · · · · · · ·

PAUSE. Sit silently and reverently with the Lord and invite him to make his presence known to you during this prayerfully reflective experience.

READ. Read the parable of Jesus a few times, either silently or aloud. Begin to notice what words and/or phrases pop off the page and land in your heart.

PONDER. Meditate on the parable, lingering with each word on the page. Note what's being formed in your heart and mind around the meaning of the parable.

PRAY. Formulate a prayer based on what you're noticing in the parable. Pay particular attention to the prompting of the Spirit toward one aspect of the parable.

REFLECT. Hold the parable like a diamond or a prism, looking at it from as many angles as possible. Notice any nuance or texture to the parable that feels invitational.

LIVE. Incarnate the truth you've discovered for your life today. Ask the Lord if there is one aspect of today's parable that you need to emulate in your sphere of influence. Or simply receive the parable as a gift for your soul.

THE OBEDIENT SERVANT

Luke 17:7-10

"Suppose one of you has a servant who comes in from plowing the field or tending the sheep. Would you take his coat, set the table, and say, 'Sit down and eat'? Wouldn't you be more likely to say, 'Prepare dinner; change your clothes and wait table for me until I've finished my coffee; then go to the kitchen and have your supper'? Does the servant get special thanks for doing what's expected of him? It's the same with you. When you've done everything expected of you, be matter-of-fact and say, 'The work is done. What we were told to do, we did.'"

VISIO DIVINA

PAUSE. Making time to be attentive, welcome the Lord to be with you while you look at this drawing, *Servant Bells*.

SEE. How does this rendering of servant bells invite curiosity and interest in the concept of servanthood? Imagine the sound and the movement of these bells calling you to serve your master. Now imagine if this sound and sight were central to your everyday work and identity.

PONDER. How is the notion of servanthood either true or foreign to your experience in life? What people, stories, or experiences have helped you better understand a life of service?

PRAY. Talk to Jesus about what you are noticing. Listen to his desire for you.

REFLECT. What comes up for you as you reflect on what it means to be a devoted servant to a loving, good Lord? What do you wrestle with? What are you grateful for?

LIVE. What next consideration seems important for you to put into practice?

SERVANT BELLS

39

THE PERSISTENT WIDOW

Luke 18:1-8

. . . .

Also known as the parable of the unjust judge, this story highlights the need for justice in the face of indifference or opposition. The widow keeps coming to the judge with a plea: "My rights are being violated. Protect me!" (Luke 18:3). Her persistence finally gets the judge's attention and leads to action.

SIMILE. The unwavering faith of the widow is matched by her consistent and persistent appeal to the unjust judge, which is likened to the prayer life Jesus is urging the disciples to embrace. It's no surprise that Jesus would use the story of a widow to illustrate his priorities. Left alone in this world, the widow pleads for justice, mercy, and protection.

CONTRAST. The faith of the persistent widow and the carelessness of the unjust judge provide a significant distinction. Jesus tells this story to assure his disciples that when the widow cries for help, she ultimately receives her request. How much more than an unjust judge will God do for those who love him? The just Judge, Jesus, delights to step into our daily fray and offer compassion, justice, and grace.

LECTIO DIVINA

PAUSE. Sit silently and reverently with the Lord and invite him to make his presence known to you during this prayerfully reflective experience.

READ. Read the parable of Jesus a few times, either silently or aloud. Begin to notice what words and/or phrases pop off the page and land in your heart.

PONDER. Meditate on the parable, lingering with each word on the page. Note what's being formed in your heart and mind around the meaning of the parable.

PRAY. Formulate a prayer based on what you're noticing in the parable. Pay particular attention to the prompting of the Spirit toward one aspect of the parable.

REFLECT. Hold the parable like a diamond or a prism, looking at it from as many angles as possible. Notice any nuance or texture to the parable that feels invitational.

LIVE. Incarnate the truth you've discovered for your life today. Ask the Lord if there is one aspect of today's parable that you need to emulate in your sphere of influence. Or simply receive the parable as a gift for your soul.

THE PERSISTENT WIDOW

Luke 18:1-8

Jesus told them a story showing that it was necessary for them to pray consistently and never quit. He said, "There was once a judge in some city who never gave God a thought and cared nothing for people. A widow in that city kept after him: 'My rights are being violated. Protect me!'

"He never gave her the time of day. But after this went on and on he said to himself, 'I care nothing what God thinks, even less what people think. But because this widow won't quit badgering me, I'd better do something and see that she gets justice—otherwise I'm going to end up beaten black-and-blue by her pounding.'"

Then the Master said, "Do you hear what that judge, corrupt as he is, is saying? So what makes you think God won't step in and work justice for his chosen people, who continue to cry out for help? Won't he stick up for them? I assure you, he will. He will not drag his feet. But how much of that kind of persistent faith will the Son of Man find on the earth when he returns?"

VISIO DIVINA

· · · · · · · · ·

PAUSE. Continue in a prayerful posture and open yourself to God's Spirit as you consider this drawing, *Cry of the Heart*.

SEE. What the judge sees is the widow's persistence. What God sees is her heart. What do you see as you linger with the artwork?

PONDER. What is the cry of *your* heart? What is a situation in your life that draws you into prayer? What prayer do you seem to be praying many times over? Do you pray often for justice with a heart of compassion and mercy?

PRAY. Take the cry of your heart once more to the God who hears and sees.

REFLECT. What happens in prayer? What is prayer for? Do you allow prayer to shape you and change your perspective? Is prayer a space where your faith is strengthened? Is prayer a place that moves you to do more or be more?

LIVE. How is Jesus inviting you to grow in a life of persistent prayer?

CRY OF THE HEART

40

THE PHARISEE AND THE TAX COLLECTOR

Luke 18:9-14

. . . .

In the Temple, the Jews' central location of worship, Jesus is directing attention to the self-righteous. At this time, they are known for their strict observance of the law and frequently consider themselves morally and religiously superior to other people. Posing in prayer, the Pharisees look down on robbers, crooks, adulterers, and even this lone quiet, humble tax man.

SIMILE. Two men go up to pray in the Temple. One is expressing prayer in worldly fashion, showing off, standing up to be noticed and heard by all. The other stands at a distance, looks up to heaven, beats his breast, and cries out for God's mercy. The tax collector is fully cognizant of his sinfulness and his desperate need for the grace of God.

CONTRAST. The self-righteous Pharisee stands in stark contrast to the brokenness and humility of the tax collector. Jesus is using these distinctions as examples of how we can choose to pray. The Pharisee is obviously puffed up with pride in his prayers. The tax collector, however, is aware of his brokenness, beating his breast in sorrow as he cries out for God's mercy.

LECTIO DIVINA

PAUSE. Sit silently and reverently with the Lord and invite him to make his presence known to you during this prayerfully reflective experience.

READ. Read the parable of Jesus a few times, either silently or aloud. Begin to notice what words and/or phrases pop off the page and land in your heart.

PONDER. Meditate on the parable, lingering with each word on the page. Note what's being formed in your heart and mind around the meaning of the parable.

PRAY. Formulate a prayer based on what you're noticing in the parable. Pay particular attention to the prompting of the Spirit toward one aspect of the parable.

REFLECT. Hold the parable like a diamond or a prism, looking at it from as many angles as possible. Notice any nuance or texture to the parable that feels invitational.

LIVE. Incarnate the truth you've discovered for your life today. Ask the Lord if there is one aspect of today's parable that you need to emulate in your sphere of influence. Or simply receive the parable as a gift for your soul.

THE PHARISEE AND THE TAX COLLECTOR

Luke 18:9-14

He told his next story to some who were complacently pleased with themselves over their moral performance and looked down their noses at the common people: "Two men went up to the Temple to pray, one a Pharisee, the other a tax man. The Pharisee posed and prayed like this: 'Oh, God, I thank you that I am not like other people—robbers, crooks, adulterers, or, heaven forbid, like this tax man. I fast twice a week and tithe on all my income.'

"Meanwhile the tax man, slumped in the shadows, his face in his hands, not daring to look up, said, 'God, give mercy. Forgive me, a sinner.'"

Jesus commented, "This tax man, not the other, went home made right with God. If you walk around with your nose in the air, you're going to end up flat on your face, but if you're content to be simply yourself, you will become more than yourself."

VISIO DIVINA

PAUSE. Lean on Jesus to guide you as you pray with this drawing, *Reflections*.

SEE. Look for the reflections that represent mirror images of pride and humility. How do the figures in the story respond to their reflections? How does their behavior mirror the condition of each of their hearts?

PONDER. Ask yourself, *How does my behavior mirror the posture of my heart?*

PRAY. In a spirit of confession and repentance, talk to Jesus about your honest acknowledgments.

REFLECT. As you come to God with a true sense of your need for forgiveness, also remember the amazing sacrifice Christ made for you on the cross. Out of gratitude for his great mercy, we can simply rest in his love rather than strive for greatness.

LIVE. How will you live humbly today as his dearly loved child?

REFLECTIONS

Conclusion and Response

"This is the Great Reversal:
many of the first ending up last, and the last first."
MATTHEW 19:30

In the Gospels, stories and images are Jesus' preferred style of communication. We glean much about the heart of God from emulating the life and teachings of our humble Lord and Savior, Jesus Christ. The creativity of Jesus invites us into our own reflective process. Time and culture notwithstanding, we are faced today with the same choices as the early disciples.

The parables are a great place to prayerfully reflect. Each one is a teachable moment for all who have ears that hear and a hunger to know God intimately in Jesus. Praying it slant is a subversive way for Jesus to make himself known and to deepen the understanding of the Kingdom of Heaven for all his most devoted followers—including you. Because it's oblique, the style of Jesus' parables is natural, conversational, and relational. As we've inclined our ear in God's direction in prayer, we've seen the fingerprints of God everywhere.

In this hands-on practice text, our hope as creators is that you've experienced the richness of the Word of God as the primary informant of your life of prayer and prayerfulness—specifically that the values and ethos of the parables have taught you a form of prayer that's simple, natural, ordinary, and daily. How are you finding yourself praying differently as a result of the practices of lectio and visio divina?

The parables of Jesus are replete with pictures of contrast: self-centered worldly-mindedness or God-centered Kingdom-mindfulness. Each parable invites a response, mostly toward a radical departure from one's normal, self-protecting idea or impulse. Each parable invites a deeper affection and unhurried intimacy with Jesus.

To notice, discern, pray, and work into your life the words of King Jesus and his Kingdom, however, is to walk faithfully with Jesus all your days. The last will be first. The least will receive the most. The smallest is actually the greatest. The lost will be found. The morsel will be multiplied. The seed must first die in the ground before it lives to produce a crop.

To all who have ears that hear: Pray it slant, and live humbly, abundantly, and fruitfully in the Kingdom of Heaven now and forever. Keep praying the parables of Jesus. Pass along the joy to others. Give God all the glory!

In the love of the Father, his beloved Son, Jesus, and the Spirit who is holy, Amen.

Acknowledgments

We are grateful to God for all the incredible support we've received for this life-giving project and for the joy we've shared in collaborating throughout the creative process. We both felt a distinct calling to this initiative, mostly out of our love for Jesus and his deeply meaningful parables. We have been challenged and convicted by the importance of understanding the parables as much more than sweet Sunday school stories. Instead, we are compelled by the seriousness with which Jesus speaks of his Kingdom. And we trust that all our readers and fellow prayers of the parables will experience a Spirit-led invitation to a reflective and unhurried intimacy with our Savior.

Thank you to our spouses, Joel Skinner and Ruth Macchia, for your loving encouragement and consistent affirmation. Your counsel and prayers are always received with grateful hearts. Our respective children and grandchildren have shared our joy, and we offer this book to them as one tangible sign of our deep and abiding affection for each of them.

To our colleagues and friends at Leadership Transformations, thank you for sharing in our excitement for this book. You mean the world to us, and we love doing ministry life with you. Your kindness and grace are examples of Kingdom life that Jesus smiles upon, and for that we are truly grateful.

Blessings to the NavPress/Tyndale team, especially David Zimmerman and Olivia Eldredge. We have been profoundly enlivened by your visionary leadership on our behalf every step of the way.

To God alone belongs all the glory, honor, and praise. We acknowledge his abiding presence in our lives, and we pray his blessing on the work of our hands and the prayers of our hearts. May the ever-expanding Kingdom heart of Jesus become ours as well as we tune our ears to hear his voice and turn our eyes to see the grandeur of his Kingdom all around us.

In the grace and peace of Christ,
Suz Skinner and Steve Macchia

About the Authors

. . . .

S. K. "Suz" Skinner

Suz Skinner's life has been a tapestry of three vocations woven together—artist, teacher, and minister of spiritual formation. She has taught and served in the contexts of university and seminary campuses, church staff teams, spiritual retreats, independent schools, her personal art studio, and the great outdoors. Currently serving as a spiritual director and faculty for Leadership Transformations, Inc., Suz's passion is to provide safe, creative space for others to meet with God and grow as his dearly loved children. Her greatest delights, shared with her husband, Joel, are two grown daughters, their remarkable husbands, and five cherished grandchildren (and always a couple of black Labradors found in the mix). To join Suz and learn more, visit skskinner.com.

Stephen A. Macchia

Steve Macchia is the founder and president of Leadership Transformations, Inc., a ministry he and his wife, Ruth, founded on July 1, 2003. Today LTI has been richly blessed by God and focuses on the spiritual formation, discernment, and renewal of leaders and learners worldwide. Over the past forty-seven years of his ministry career, he has also served as a member of the pastoral team at Grace Chapel in Lexington, Massachusetts; the president of Vision New England (formerly known as the Evangelistic Association of New England); and the director of the Pierce Center for Disciple Building at Gordon-Conwell Theological Seminary. He currently teaches in the doctor of ministry program at Gordon-Conwell in the Spiritual Formation for Ministry Leaders cohort. Steve is the author or coauthor of seventeen books, including the Baker bestseller *Becoming a Healthy Church* as well as *Becoming a Healthy Disciple, Becoming a Healthy Team, Crafting a Rule of Life, Broken and Whole,* and *The Discerning Life*. He is also the creator of the Church Health Assessment Tool (CHAT) and the Team Health Assessment Tool (THAT). Steve is the proud father of two grown children, is grateful for their much-beloved spouses, and loves being Papa to his three precious grandchildren. More information about Steve can be found at stevemacchia.com and leadershiptransformations.org.

About Leadership Transformations, Inc.

Christian leaders often feel overwhelmed trying to keep up with the high demands of life, leadership, and relationships. Unfortunately, it's difficult to find relevant spiritual and practical training to help them grow and thrive in their faith and leadership. That's why, for more than twenty years, Leadership Transformations, Inc. has trained thousands of leaders and learners from all walks of life in ancient spiritual practices that help them slow down, listen, and discern the voice of God. As a result, they live lives of formation, discernment, and renewal.

From its inception in 2003, LTI has been an important part of the spiritual formation community by serving, teaching, and coaching leaders across the globe and guiding them into a deeper, more intimate walk with Christ. We believe that when leaders have the right resources to help them experience a deep and refreshing connection to God they are positioned to become Spirit-empowered leaders who are transforming their communities and advancing the Kingdom of God.

Vision

LTI's vision is for local churches and Christian organizations to be filled with leaders and learners who place spiritual formation, discernment, and renewal above all other leadership priorities.

Mission

LTI's mission is to cultivate vibrant spirituality and attentive discernment among Christian leaders and teams. To accomplish this mission, the staff, volunteers, and board members, together with strategic partners, create formal and informal opportunities for leaders and teams to

- embrace a lifestyle of Sabbath rest and renewal;
- experience spiritual reflection, biblical truth, and attentive discernment;
- acknowledge the Holy Spirit's constant presence and work in their lives;
- attend to new insights with open-handed receptivity and initiative; and
- sense a renewed invitation to discover God's call on their lives and ministries.

Resources and Offerings

Abide: Certificate in Spiritual Formation
Emmaus: Certificate in Formational Leadership
Selah: Certificate in Spiritual Direction
Online Workshops and Retreats
The Discerning Leader Podcast
PATHWAYS Weekly Newsletter
Soul-Care Retreats and Soul Sabbaths
Spiritual Discernment for Teams
Sabbatical Planning and Coaching
Spiritual Health Assessments:
- Church Health Assessment Tool (healthychurch.net)
- Team Health Assessment Tool (leadershiptransformations.org/team-health)
Crafting a Rule of Life (ruleoflife.com)
Online Store (spiritualformationstore.com)

leadershiptransformations.org

Notes

1. Emily Dickinson, "Tell All the Truth but Tell It Slant," in *The Poems of Emily Dickinson: Reading Edition* (The Belknap Press of Harvard University Press, 1999).
2. Eugene H. Peterson, *Tell It Slant: A Conversation on the Language of Jesus in His Stories and Prayers* (Eerdmans, 2008), 3.
3. Dickinson, "Tell All the Truth."
4. Peterson, *Tell It Slant*, 4.
5. Peterson, *Tell It Slant*, 19–20.
6. Eugene H. Peterson, *The Message Prayerful Reading Bible* (NavPress, 2022), A15–A16.
7. Peterson, *The Message Prayerful Reading Bible*, A9.
8. These six steps are adapted from Peterson, *The Message Prayerful Reading Bible*, A17.
9. Joan Huyser-Honig, "Visio Divina: Sacred Seeing to Encounter God," Calvin Institute of Christian Worship, November 3, 2021, https://worship.calvin.edu/resources/articles/visio-divina-sacred-seeing-encounter-god.
10. Peterson, *Tell It Slant*, 20–21.
11. Stephen A. Macchia, *Path of a Beloved Disciple: 31 Days in the Gospel of John* (LTI Publications, 2014).